My Google
Chromebook™
THIRD EDITION

Michael Miller

que®

800 East 96th Street,
Indianapolis, Indiana 46240 USA

My Google Chromebook™, Third Edition

ISBN-13: 978-0-7897-5534-6
ISBN-10: 0-7897-5534-3

Library of Congress Control Number: 2015941258

Printed in the United States of America

First Printing: August 2015

Trademarks

All terms mentioned in this book that are known to be trademarks or service marks have been appropriately capitalized. Que Publishing cannot attest to the accuracy of this information. Use of a term in this book should not be regarded as affecting the validity of any trademark or service mark.

Warning and Disclaimer

Every effort has been made to make this book as complete and as accurate as possible, but no warranty or fitness is implied. The information provided is on an "as is" basis. The author and the publisher shall have neither liability nor responsibility to any person or entity with respect to any loss or damages arising from the information contained in this book.

Special Sales

For information about buying this title in bulk quantities, or for special sales opportunities (which may include electronic versions; custom cover designs; and content particular to your business, training goals, marketing focus, or branding interests), please contact our corporate sales department at corpsales@pearsoned.com or (800) 382-3419.

For government sales inquiries, please contact governmentsales@pearsoned.com.

For questions about sales outside the U.S., please contact international@pearsoned.com.

Editor-in-Chief
Greg Wiegand

Executive Editor
Rick Kughen

Development Editor
Joyce Nielsen

Managing Editor
Sandra Schroeder

Project Editor
Mandie Frank

Copy Editor
Bart Reed

Senior Indexer
Cheryl Lenser

Proofreader
Paula Lowell

Technical Editor
Karen Weinstein

Editorial Assistant
Kristen Watterson

Designer
Mark Shirar

Compositor
Nonie Ratcliff

Contents at a Glance

Bonus Chapters! There are four additional chapters and a task available to you at www.quepublishing.com/title/9780789755346. Click the Downloads tab to access the links to download the PDF files.

Table of Contents

Formatting Documents 228

    Format Text 228

    Format a Paragraph 229

    Apply Styles 230

Printing and Sharing Documents 230

    Print a Document 230

    Share a Document with Others 231

16 Spreadsheets with Google Sheets   **235**

Getting to Know Google Sheets 235

    Navigate the Google Sheets Dashboard 236

    Navigate Google Sheets 237

Working with Spreadsheets 237

    Open an Existing Spreadsheet 238

    Create a New Spreadsheet 238

    Import an Excel File 239

    Export a Spreadsheet to Excel 240

Entering and Editing Data 241

    Enter Data 241

    Edit Cell Data 241

    Select Rows and Columns 242

    Work with Sheets and Tabs 242

Formatting Cells and Data 243

    Format Cell Data 243

    Format Numbers 244

    Format Cell Color 245

    Format Cell Borders 245

Working with Formulas and Functions 246

    Entering a Formula 246

    Using Functions 248

Creating Charts 250

    Create a Basic Chart 250

    Select a Different Chart Type 252

    Customize a Chart 252

Printing and Sharing Spreadsheets 253

    Print a Spreadsheet 253

    Share a Spreadsheet with Others 255

Bonus Chapters! There are four additional chapters and a task available to you at www.quepublishing.com/title/9780789755346. Click the Downloads tab to access the links to download the PDF files.

About the Author

Michael Miller is a prolific and popular writer of more than 150 nonfiction books, known for his ability to explain complex topics to everyday readers. He writes about a variety of topics, including technology, business, and music. His best-selling books for Que include *Easy Computer Basics, Computer Basics: Absolute Beginner's Guide, My Facebook for Seniors*, and *Googlepedia: The Ultimate Google Resource*. Worldwide, his books have sold more than 1 million copies.

Find out more at the author's website: www.millerwriter.com

Follow the author on Twitter: @molehillgroup

Dedication

To my wonderful grandkids Alethia, Collin, Hayley, Judah, Lael, and Jackson.

Acknowledgments

Thanks to all the folks at Que who helped turned this manuscript into a book, including Rick Kughen, Greg Wiegand, Mandie Frank, Joyce Nielsen, Bart Reed, and technical editor Karen Weinstein.

We Want to Hear from You!

As the reader of this book, *you* are our most important critic and commentator. We value your opinion and want to know what we're doing right, what we could do better, what areas you'd like to see us publish in, and any other words of wisdom you're willing to pass our way.

We welcome your comments. You can email or write to let us know what you did or didn't like about this book—as well as what we can do to make our books better.

Please note that we cannot help you with technical problems related to the topic of this book.

When you write, please be sure to include this book's title and author as well as your name and email address. We will carefully review your comments and share them with the author and editors who worked on the book.

Email: feedback@quepublishing.com

Mail: Que Publishing
ATTN: Reader Feedback
800 East 96th Street
Indianapolis, IN 46240 USA

Reader Services

Visit our website and register this book at quepublishing.com/register for convenient access to any updates, downloads, or errata that might be available for this book.

HP Chromebook 14

In this chapter, you will learn about web-based computing with Google's Chrome OS running on Chromebook computers.

→ What Is a Chromebook?
→ What Is Google Chrome OS?
→ What Is Cloud Computing?
→ Should You Buy a Chromebook?
→ What Chromebook Should You Buy?

Understanding Chrome OS, Chromebooks, and Cloud Computing

A Chromebook is a popular type of notebook computer that's not a Mac and not a Windows PC. Instead, Chromebooks run Google's Chrome operating system—Chrome OS—a newer type of web-based operating system.

Chromebooks come in a variety of types and sizes, but all are lightweight and have very long battery life. They don't have much in the way of internal storage, but they don't need it; all of your files are stored online, in web-based storage.

All you need to run your Chromebook and access your files is an Internet connection. In fact, you can access your files from anywhere, even from other Chromebooks, because they're not stored locally. It's all about what's called *cloud computing*, which uses applications and data files stored in the "cloud" of the Internet, not on any individual personal computer.

Because of its web-based nature, using a Chromebook and the Chrome OS is quite a bit different from using a traditional notebook PC and either Microsoft Windows or the Mac OS. To get the most use out of your new Chromebook, then, you need to become familiar with how cloud computing works—as well as all the ins and outs of your new Chromebook.

What Is a Chromebook?

Put simply, a Chromebook is a notebook computer that runs the Google Chrome OS. Whereas most notebooks run a version of the Microsoft Windows or Mac OS operating systems, Chromebooks instead run Google's web-based operating system (hence the name Chromebook—a notebook running Google Chrome OS).

Acer Chromebook 13

Most Chromebooks are smaller and lighter than traditional notebook PCs. Because most Chromebooks don't contain a hard disk or CD/DVD drive, that space and weight is removed from the equation. Most Chromebooks have 12"–15" (or so) diagonal screens, are very thin, and weigh less than three pounds.

Chromebox

Chromebooks are portable computers. If you want a desktop computer that runs the Chrome OS, look for what is called a Chromebox. ASUS makes just such a computer (called the ASUS Chromebox) that sells for $179—keyboard and mouse included, monitor extra.

If there's no hard drive inside, how does a Chromebook store your data? The answer is *solid state storage*, the same kind you find on USB flash drives and the memory cards you use with your digital camera. Most current Chromebooks come with 16GB or 32GB of internal solid state storage—considerably less than what you find on a traditional notebook's hard drive, but all that Chrome OS needs to run. As for storing your data, that's what the Web is for; a Chromebook needs only minimal local storage.

In terms of processing power, today's Chromebooks use one of several dual- or quad-core processors. Intel and NVIDIA chips power most Chromebooks today, although Samsung uses its own proprietary processor for its Chromebook models.

This combination of small screen, minimal solid state storage, and efficient processor means that a Chromebook has an impressive battery life—typically 8 hours or more on a charge, and up to 12 hours for those models with the new Celeron Bay Trail-M chip. Chromebooks are also virtually instant on, booting up in less than 10 seconds, and resuming instantly from sleep mode. It's a much different—and much more efficient—computing experience than what you're used to.

In essence, then, a Chromebook is a computer that is built and optimized for the Web, using Chrome OS. This provides a faster, simplified, and more secure computing environment than with traditional Windows or Mac computers.

Chromebooks Online

Learn more about Chromebooks and Google Chrome OS online at www.google.com/chromebook/.

What Is Google Chrome OS?

Google's Chrome OS is the world's first operating system for the new era of cloud computing. It's a web-based operating system, in that it relies on a variety of web-based services and applications to work; it doesn't run traditional desktop applications. It's designed to be used on smallish computers that are wirelessly connected to the Internet.

Because it runs over the Web, Chrome OS is a "lightweight" operating system, in that it doesn't have a large footprint in terms of file size or memory or processing requirements. It can fit quite easily within the limited internal storage space of a small Chromebook computer, and is automatically updated whenever the computer is connected to the Internet. It's also relatively fast and efficient, which results in short startup times and sprightly operation.

Chrome and Linux

Chrome is an open source operating system, which means that it can be freely distributed without paying expensive licensing costs. It is based on a version of Linux, another operating system that itself is based on the established UNIX operating system. The Chrome OS interface runs on top of the underlying Linux kernel.

The Chrome OS running on Chromebooks today isn't what users saw on the initial Chromebooks that shipped way back in 2011. That first iteration of Chrome OS closely resembled Google's Chrome web browser. There was no traditional desktop, as found in Microsoft Windows or Apple's Mac OS, and applications were launched in individual tabs within the Chrome browser. Using this early version of Chrome was more like browsing the Web than it was navigating a complex operating system, such as Windows.

People didn't like that browser-based interface, so Google changed it. The current version of Chrome OS features the same sort of desktop you find in Windows or the Mac OS. Applications open in their own multiple windows on the desktop, and you can easily switch from one open window to another. It's very similar to using Microsoft Windows or the Mac OS; the big difference is that most of what you launch is housed on the Web, not locally.

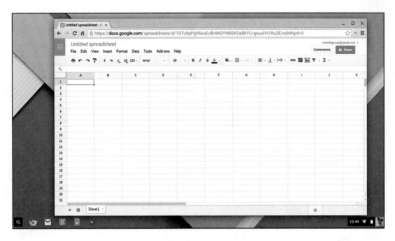

The Chrome OS desktop

That's right, Chrome OS does not and cannot run traditional software programs; everything it runs must be a web-based application. This means that you can't use software programs such as Microsoft Office or Adobe Photoshop, just web-based apps. (Although many companies—including Microsoft and Adobe—are introducing web-based versions of their traditional software programs.)

That's not necessarily a bad thing. Using web-based applications—or what we call *cloud computing*—has a lot of benefits, as we'll discuss next.

What Is Cloud Computing?

Cloud computing represents a major shift in how we run computer applications and store data. With cloud computing, instead of applications and data being hosted on an individual desktop computer, everything is hosted in the "cloud"—a nebulous assemblage of computers and servers accessed via the Internet. Cloud computing lets you access your applications and documents from anywhere in the world, freeing you from the confines of the desktop and facilitating wholesale group collaboration.

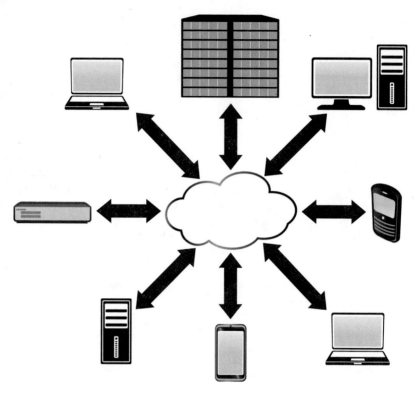

Cloud computing connects various types of devices to a central "cloud" where applications and documents reside.

How Traditional Desktop Computing Works

Traditional desktop computing is all about the sovereignty of the individual computer. Although individual computers can be networked together, all the computer power resides on the desktop; each personal computer has its own massive amounts of memory and hard disk storage.

This storage is put to good use, to store all your programs and data. You have to install on your computer a copy of each software program you use. These programs are run from your computer's hard drive, and the documents you create are stored on the same computer and hard drive. Programs and documents are specific to individual machines.

In other words, desktop computing is computer-centric.

How Cloud Computing Works

In contrast, cloud computing doesn't depend on individual computers much at all. With cloud computing, the applications you run and the documents you create aren't stored on your personal computer, but are rather stored on servers accessed via the Internet. If your computer crashes, the application is still available for others to use—or for you to run from another computer.

It's the same thing with the documents you create, but even more so. Because the documents are stored in the "cloud," anyone with permission not only can access the documents but can also edit and collaborate on those documents in real time.

Unlike traditional computing, then, this cloud computing model isn't computer-centric, it's user- or document-centric. Which computer you use to access a document simply isn't important; instead, the focus is on your apps and data, which can be accessed from anywhere, on any device—such as a Chromebook or Chromebox PC.

>>>Go Further
DEFINING THE CLOUD

Key to the definition of cloud computing is the "cloud" itself. Put simply, the cloud is a grid of interconnected computers. These computers can be personal computers or network servers; they can be public or private.

For example, Google hosts a cloud that consists of both smallish PCs and larger servers. Google's cloud is a private one (that is, Google owns it) that is publicly accessible (by Google's users).

This cloud of computers extends beyond a single company or enterprise. The applications and data served by the cloud are available to a broad group of users, cross-enterprise and cross-platform. Access is via the Internet; any authorized user can access these docs and apps from any computer over any Internet connection. And, to the user, the technology and infrastructure behind the cloud is invisible; all you see are the applications and documents you use, not the technology that drives access.

Should You Buy a Chromebook?

Chromebooks both define and depend on cloud computing to work. All the apps you run and all the files you create are stored on the Web, and accessed via the Internet on your Google Chrome device.

Samsung Chromebook 2

But Chromebooks aren't the only type of computing devices that rely on cloud computing. Smartphones and tablets are much like Chromebooks (but without the keyboard) in that they have minimal internal storage, instead storing all their data on the Web. And although they may store many of their apps locally, there's still a lot of cloud streaming going on.

For this reason, people use Chromebooks for many of the same tasks they do on their iPads or other tablets. Watching streaming video from the cloud is a snap with a Chromebook, as is listening to streaming music, viewing your Facebook or Twitter feed, and the like. The fact that you have a keyboard attached just makes the Chromebook that much more versatile.

If you think a full-fledged computer sounds better than a tablet (and many do), a Chromebook is a good choice. But Chromebooks aren't the only low-priced computers around. Starting in 2014, Microsoft began encouraging PC manufacturers to release small Windows-based notebooks in the Chromebook price range—as low as $250 or so. So while Chromebooks used to have the price advantage, now they compete with similarly priced computers that run Windows and traditional Windows apps.

This begs the question—is a Chromebook the right device for you? Or should you invest in a tablet or a low-priced Windows PC?

As with any technology purchase, you need to weigh the pros and cons, and then decide what's best for your own personal use. With that in mind, let's take a look at the benefits and disadvantages you might find in using a Chromebook running Chrome OS.

Chromebook vs. Tablet

For many users, a Chromebook is a viable alternative to purchasing an iPad or similar tablet computer. There are many advantages to using a Chromebook over a tablet, including the following:

- **Keyboard and touchpad**—A tablet is just a screen—a touchscreen, mind you, but a screen nonetheless. If you want to do anything beyond watching movies and browsing web pages, it's difficult; you have to tap an onscreen virtual keyboard, which isn't that great for anything more than a tweet or a short Facebook post. A Chromebook, on the other hand, includes a traditional computer keyboard and mouse-like touchpad, both of which are necessary if you need to input much of anything at all. Given the similar price, that keyboard and touchpad add tremendous value to a Chromebook.

- **More productivity**—The Chromebook's keyboard and mouse input let you be a lot more productive than you can on a tablet. Whether you're writing school essays or business reports, you need that keyboard. Same thing if you do a lot of emailing or number crunching; you just can't do it as well or as accurately on a tablet's onscreen keyboard. The touchpad is also useful if you're doing heavy-duty photo editing or serious game play. In other words, if it's productivity you're looking for, a Chromebook is the way to go.

- **Inputs and outputs**—Some tablets have a USB port or two, but many (including the best-selling Apple iPad) don't. That's where a Chromebook shines. In terms of connectors, it's outfitted like a traditional notebook PC. There are some differences between models, but expect to find at least two USB input/output ports and an HDMI output. The USB ports let you connect USB flash drives, external storage devices, and peripherals; the HDMI port provides high-definition audio/video output to a widescreen TV or home theater system. You don't get all this with a typical tablet.

- **Bigger screen**—Tablets today come in two primary screen sizes—small (8" or so) and large (10" or so). Small tablets typically cost about the same as a Chromebook, in the $200–$250 range, but with a much smaller screen. And the larger tablets, although much more expensive, aren't that much larger—and still smaller than a Chromebook screen. If you need the screen real estate, whether for watching movies or browsing websites, the Chromebook is the choice for you.

- **Price**—With numerous options in the $199–$299 price range, Chromebooks are price-competitive with the lower-end tablets such as the small-screen Google Nexus 7 and Apple iPad Mini. Of course, you get a lot more for the money with the Chromebook—bigger screen, keyboard, touchpad, input/output ports, and so on. The price comparison is even more skewed when you compare a Chromebook with the higher-priced tablets, such as the full-sized Apple iPad. For the price of an iPad ($400 and up) you can buy two Chromebooks—or just one and have money left over for more fun stuff.

In other words, a Chromebook gives you all the productivity and connectivity of a notebook computer, but in a tablet-like form factor and price point. If you're comparing a Chromebook to a tablet, you can do a lot more with the Chromebook.

>>>Go Further

CHROMEBOOKS IN EDUCATION

When Apple released its first iPad tablet, it got a tremendous response from the education market. Schools across the country and around the world recognized how easy using the iPad was, and how they could use it to teach technology to their students.

It didn't take long, however, for schools to recognize the iPad's limitations. First, the lack of a keyboard made it more difficult to do input-heavy tasks. Second, Apple's closed infrastructure made it difficult to manage large numbers of iPads in a typical school installation. And third, there's the cost— at $400 or more a pop, equipping every student with an iPad is a pricey proposition.

This explains why more and more school districts have been trading in their iPads for Google Chromebooks. More than 10,000 schools in the U.S. now use Chromebooks—up from just 5,000 schools six months ago. In fact, Google now owns close to 50% of the K-12 school market, easily surpassing Apple's share.

Why do schools like Chromebooks? It's for all the reasons they no longer fancy iPads. Chromebooks are true productivity devices, thanks to the built-in keyboard and bigger screen. They're easier to manage across a school or school district because the entire OS is web based. They're a lot, lot lower priced than Apple's tablets. And any student can use any Chromebook; as a "zero state" device, any student can log on to any Chromebook with their personal account and see their own desktop and apps. (iPads, on the other hand, are inextricably linked to a single user account.)

And it's not just the bureaucrats and IT folks who like Chromebooks. Students overwhelmingly prefer the laptop form factor over that of tablets. It's a lot easier to search Google, write papers, and even enter programming code on a real keyboard than on a touchscreen.

For these reasons and more, Google is winning the hearts and minds of teachers and students across the country. Chances are that the children in your neighborhood are familiar with Chromebooks—and like them!

Chromebook vs. Traditional Notebook

A Chromebook is also a viable alternative to a traditional Windows or Mac notebook PC. There are a lot of advantages to the Chromebook in this comparison, including the following:

- **Low price**—Although some Windows PCs sell in the sub-$300 range, most traditional notebooks will set you back $500 or more (much more, in terms of Apple products). When you want a second device for consuming media or casual productivity, the low cost of a Chromebook is very appealing.

- **No software to buy**—Not only does a Chromebook cost less than a comparable Windows or Mac notebook, you also don't have to lay out big bucks for software to run on the device. Because a Chromebook doesn't run traditional (and expensive) computer software, you instead load a variety of free or low-cost web-based apps. Considering the high price of Microsoft Office and similar programs, you can save hundreds or even thousands of dollars by using web-based applications instead. That also means you don't have to worry about installing multiple programs, or managing regular upgrades; with web apps there's nothing to install, and all upgrades happen automatically.

- **No worry about local storage and backup**—With a traditional computer you have to manage limited hard disk storage space and worry about backing up your important files. Not so with a Chromebook; all your files are stored on the Web, where you have virtually unlimited storage, so you don't have to worry about data storage at all. You also don't have to worry about backups, because you always have a copy of your files online.

- **Reduced malware danger**—Because you don't download and run traditional computer software, computer viruses and spyware are virtual non-issues on a Chromebook. You don't even have to run antivirus programs, because viruses simply can't be installed on Chrome OS.

- **Enhanced security**—If you lose a traditional computer, all your personal files and information is also lost—or, in the case of theft, placed in the hands of criminals. Not so with a Chromebook. If somebody steals your Chromebook, all they get is a piece of hardware; because all files and data are stored on the Web, nothing important resides on the machine itself. This makes a Chromebook the most secure computer available today.

- **More portability**—Like a tablet, a Chromebook is smaller and lighter than a traditional notebook PC. That's great for when you're on the go.

- **Faster boot up**—Instant resumption from sleep mode. Reboot from scratch in under 10 seconds. Try to find a Windows-based computer that can do that.

- **Longer battery life**—Since Chromebooks run very efficiently (and don't have to drive CD/DVD drives and hard drives), they have significantly longer battery life than a typical notebook PC. Some of the newer Chromebooks will last 12 hours or more on a single charge, which is truly liberating when you're on the go.

- **Enhanced collaboration**—Cloud computing is built for collaboration. Because your documents are all stored on the Web, multiple users can access and edit those documents in real time. No more passing files around from user to user—all you have to do is use your Chromebook to go online and start collaborating.

- **Ideal for multiple users**—With traditional computing, every user has to have his own computer, which stores all his files and personalized computing environment. With Chrome OS, your files, applications, and personalized desktop are stored on the Web; any Chromebook you use becomes your personal Chromebook once you log in to your Google account. A single Chromebook can easily be shared between multiple users, and it really doesn't matter whose computer it is.

Put simply, a Chromebook gives you all the advantages of a tablet combined with traditional notebook PC productivity—at a very attractive price. Even when you consider a Chromebook versus a sub-$300 Windows notebook, the Chromebook still is lighter, faster, and more secure than a Windows or Mac notebook—and costs less to use, too.

HP Chromebook 14

In this chapter, you'll learn how to recognize the various pieces and parts of your new Chromebook, as well as how to use the keyboard and touchpad.

2

Getting to Know Your Chromebook

A Chromebook looks much like a traditional notebook computer. The lid opens to show the LCD display and keyboard, and there are ports and connectors and such along all sides of the case.

Before you use your Chromebook, you need to know what all these items are and what they do. You'll also want to get to know the Chromebook's keyboard and touchpad, which are a bit different from those found on other computers.

Understanding the Parts of a Chromebook

A Chromebook is like a simplified version of a traditional notebook computer. There are fewer ports and connectors, and even fewer keys on the keyboard and touchpad. That makes it easier to operate—if you know where everything is located.

Different Models, Different Manufacturers

Although the keyboard and main operating controls are similar among the different models, different manufacturers include different sets of ports on their Chromebooks—and put them in different places. Consult your Chromebook's operating manual for specific instructions.

What's Not Included

Because a Chromebook is streamlined by design, it lacks some of the connections found in a traditional Windows or Mac computer. For example, there is no Ethernet port, no CD/DVD drive, and no microphone input.

Screen

When you open the Chromebook case, the screen is the first thing you see. This is an LCD screen, typically backlit, for decent viewing even under bright light. (Some Chromebooks have touchscreens, which let you use your fingers to tap onscreen buttons and such.)

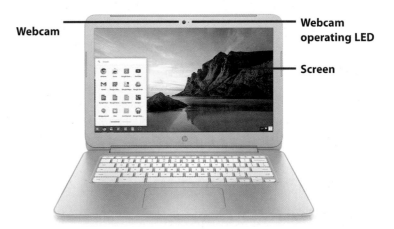

Webcam

All Chromebooks come with a built-in camera, also known as a *webcam*. The webcam is typically located directly above the screen, in the middle of the frame. You can use the webcam to conduct video chats and conferences, make video calls, create recorded videos, and take still photographs of yourself.

When you're using the webcam, the webcam's operating LED lights up. This LED is located next to the webcam, above the Chromebook's screen.

Microphone

The Chromebook's microphone is also typically located above the screen, either to the left or right of the webcam. It is used to capture audio during video chats, conferences, calls, and recordings. You can also use it for audio chats and Internet phone calls.

Keyboard

The keyboard is located on the base of the Chromebook. It's a little different from a traditional Windows or Mac keyboard, in that nonessential keys have been removed and web-specific keys have been added. Learn more about the Chromebook's keyboard in the "Using the Keyboard" section, later in this chapter.

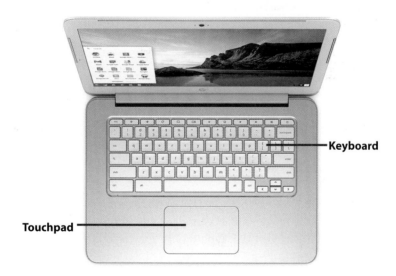

Touchpad

The Chromebook's touchpad is located directly below the primary keyboard. It functions as your Chromebook's mouse and cursor controller. Note that the touchpad does not include a right- or left-click button; instead, you tap the touchpad itself to click. Learn more in the "Using the Touchpad" section, later in this chapter.

Headset Jack

You'll find a headset jack on either the front or side of the Chromebook. Use this jack to connect a headset or earbuds for listening to your Chromebook's audio.

Memory Card Slot

Most Chromebooks include a slot for solid-state memory cards, like those used in digital cameras. This is typically a multicard slot, capable of accepting different types of cards—SD, SDHC, SDXC, Micro SD, and so forth.

Some Chromebooks put the memory card slot on the left or right side of the case, some in the rear. You can use this slot to access photos from a digital camera, MP3 audio files, or even stored video files.

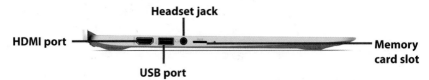

USB Ports

Chromebooks have two or more USB ports, a combination of the older USB 2.0 port and the newer USB 3.0 standard. The Google Chromebook Pixel 2 comes with the newest USB Type-C port. You can use these ports to connect any USB devices to your Chromebook.

HDMI Connector

Many Chromebooks feature an HDMI connector, typically on the rear of the unit. Use this connector to connect your Chromebook to a flat panel

TV or audio/video receiver; it transmits both HD video and audio from your Chromebook.

Status Indicator

On either the front or rear of the Chromebook you should see a small LED light that serves as a status indicator. This indicator typically glows green when the Chromebook is running on external power and the battery is fully charged; it glows red when running on external power and the battery is being charged; and it is off when the computer is running on battery power.

Power Connector

The final item on the back of most Chromebooks is the DC jack. This is where you connect the AC adapter to your Chromebook for external power.

AC/DC

Your Chromebook natively runs on DC (direct current) power, such as that supplied by the internal battery. Because the electricity from a wall outlet is AC (alternating current), the external power adapter is necessary to convert the AC power to DC power.

Using the Keyboard

The Chromebook keyboard is a simplified version of a traditional computer keyboard. It's simplified in that several lesser-used keys are missing; this lets your Chromebook make the remaining keys bigger in a smaller space.

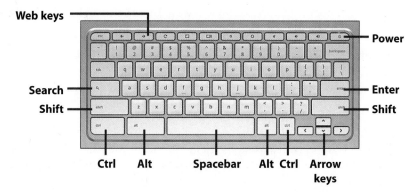

The first keys that are missing are the traditional function (F1, F2, F3, and so on) keys normally found on the top row of the keyboard. In place of these function keys, Chromebooks typically feature a row of "web keys" that perform specific functions for web browsing. The following table describes these web keys found on the top row of most Chromebook keyboards.

Web Key	Function
←	Go to the previous page in your browser history.
→	Go to the next page in your browser history.
↻	Reload the current page.
⬀	Open the current page in full-screen mode.
▭	Switch to next window.
☼	Decrease screen brightness.
✳	Increase screen brightness.
🔇	Mute/unmute the audio.
🔉	Decrease the volume.
🔊	Increase the volume.

The row of web keys also includes your Chromebook's Power button, which you use to turn your Chromebook on or off. The LED on this button shows your Chromebook's operating status: It lights on when your Chromebook is running, blinks when your Chromebook is in sleep mode, and is dark when your Chromebook is turned completely off. There's also an Esc key on the far left side of this row.

Beneath the top row of web keys is the expected row of numeric (1, 2, 3, and so on) keys. This row also includes the Backspace key, which deletes the previous character entered.

The next three rows contain the traditional alphabetic (A, B, C, and so on) keys. At the ends of these rows are your Chromebook's Shift, Ctrl, Alt, and Enter keys, along with a grouping of four arrow keys for navigation.

Note that there is no Caps Lock key on the Chromebook; if you need to type capital letters, you'll need to hold down the Shift key as necessary (at least on some models; some manufacturers go with a slightly different keyboard layout that still includes the Caps Lock key).

 Where you might expect to find a Caps Lock key is a new Chrome-specific Search key. Press this key to go to the address bar on the New Tab page to initiate a web search.

It's Not All Good

If you're used to a traditional Windows or Mac computer, you'll find several keys missing from the Chromebook keyboard. Here are the keys you're used to that aren't on the Chromebook:

- F1–F12 function keys
- Caps Lock
- Insert
- Delete
- Home

- End
- Page Down
- Page Up
- Windows
- Menu

Turn the Search Key into a Caps Lock Key

You can, with a little work, turn Chrome's Search key into a Caps Lock key. Click your profile picture at the bottom right of the screen and select Settings. When the Settings page appears, go to the Device section and click the Keyboard Settings button. When the Keyboard Settings dialog box appears, pull down the Search list and select Caps Lock. Click the OK button when done.

Using the Touchpad

Just below the keyboard is your Chromebook's touchpad, which provides the same functionality as an external mouse. That is, you use the touchpad to move the onscreen cursor and click and select items onscreen.

Touchpad ⸻

External Mouse

If you don't like the touchpad, you can connect an external mouse to one of the Chromebook's USB ports. See the "Connecting External Devices" section, later in this chapter, to learn how.

Move the Cursor

You use your finger on the touchpad to move the cursor around the Chromebook screen.

1. Place your finger lightly on the touchpad.

2. Move your finger in the direction in which you want to move the cursor.

The mouse cursor moves in the direction you moved your finger.

Click the Cursor

There are two ways to click an item onscreen, both of which utilize the touchpad.

1. Move the cursor on top of the item to click.

2. Tap your finger anywhere on the touchpad.

To double-click an item, tap twice instead of once.

Right-Click the Cursor

Many useful functions often appear via a pop-up menu when you right-click an item onscreen. But how do you right-click a touchpad that doesn't have a right button?

1. Move the cursor to the item on which you want to right-click.
2. Place two fingers anywhere on the touchpad and press once.

Drag an Item

To move an item to another position on screen, you drag it to a new position.

1. Move the cursor to the item you want to move.
2. Press and hold the touchpad while you drag the item to a new location.
3. Lift your finger from the touchpad to "drop" the item in place.

Scroll the Screen

If you're viewing a long web page or editing a long document, you need to scroll down the screen to see the entire page. Although you can do this with the keyboard's up-arrow and down-arrow keys, you can also scroll with the touchpad.

1. Place two fingers lightly on the touchpad, but do *not* press down on the touchpad.
2. Drag your fingers down to scroll down the page.
3. Drag your fingers up to scroll up the page.

>>>*Go Further*

PAGE SCROLLING

On a traditional notebook PC, you can scroll up or down one page at a time by using the Page Up and Page Down keys. Unfortunately, there are no Page Up and Page Down keys on a Chromebook keyboard, so that option is not available. You can, however, press the Alt+Up Arrow and Alt+Down Arrow key combinations to scroll up or down one page at a time. You can also press the Spacebar to scroll down a page.

Adjust Touchpad Sensitivity

If you find that your touchpad is too sensitive, or not sensitive enough, you can adjust the sensitivity of the touchpad.

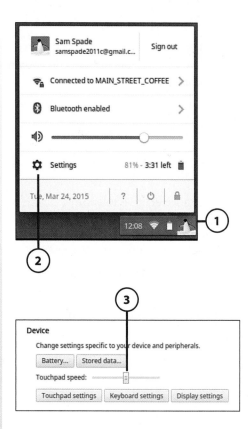

1. Click your profile picture at the bottom of the screen to display the pop-up menu.

2. Select Settings.

3. Go to the Device section and drag the Touchpad Speed slider to the left to make it less sensitive, or to the right to make it more sensitive.

Tap-to-Click

By default, you click within the touch area of the touchpad to click an onscreen item. If you'd prefer to press in the touch area instead, click the Touchpad Settings button and then uncheck the Enable Tap-to-Click box. Click OK when done.

Connecting External Devices

Although a Chromebook is a relatively self-contained unit, you can connect various external devices to the machine, typically via USB.

Connect an External Mouse

If you don't like your Chromebook's built-in touchpad, you can connect an external mouse to one of the USB ports. You can connect either a corded or cordless model.

1. Connect the cable from the external mouse to one of the Chromebook's USB ports. (If you're connecting a wireless mouse, plug the wireless receiver into the USB port.)

2. Your Chromebook should immediately recognize the external mouse and make it available for use.

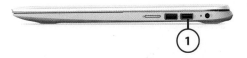

Connect an External Keyboard

You can also connect a larger external keyboard to your Chromebook via USB. As with an external mouse, you can connect either a corded or cordless keyboard.

1. Connect the cable from the external keyboard to one of the Chromebook's USB ports. (If you're connecting a wireless keyboard, plug the wireless receiver into the USB port.)

2. Your Chromebook should immediately recognize the external keyboard and make it available for use.

Connect to a Large-Screen TV

If you're watching streaming movies or television programs, the typical Chromebook screen doesn't quite deliver a big-screen viewing experience. Fortunately, you can use your Chromebook to deliver streaming Internet programming to your living room TV—and watch it all on the big screen.

1. Connect one end of an HDMI cable to the HDMI connector on your Chromebook.

2. Connect the other end of the HDMI cable to an HDMI input on your television set or audio/video receiver.

3. Switch your TV or receiver to the proper HDMI input.

You should now see on your television screen whatever is playing on your Chromebook.

External Storage

You can also connect certain external storage devices to your Chromebook via USB. Learn more in Chapter 7, "Managing Files and Using External Storage."

Adjusting Brightness and Volume

Your Chromebook includes dedicated keys, located in the top row of the keyboard, for adjusting screen brightness and audio volume.

Adjust Screen Brightness

You can make your Chromebook display brighter or darker. A brighter display may look nicer, especially under bright lighting, but can drain the battery faster. Dimming the screen a tad can still look good while maximizing battery life.

1. To increase screen brightness, press the Increase Brightness key.

2. To decrease screen brightness, press the Decrease Brightness key.

One press of either key changes the brightness by one level.

>>>Go Further

CLEANING THE SCREEN

It's important to keep your Chromebook's LCD screen clean. You should clean the screen with a soft cloth, lightly moistened with a special computer cleansing fluid. You can find this fluid at any consumer electronics or computer supply store. Squirt the fluid directly on your cleaning cloth and then lightly wipe the screen in a single direction; using too much force can damage the screen.

Adjust and Mute the Volume

Whether you're using your Chromebook's built-in speaker or listening through headphones or earbuds, you'll probably need to adjust the volume level at some point.

1. To increase the volume level, press the Increase Volume key.

2. To decrease the volume level, press the Decrease Volume key.

3. To mute the volume, press the Mute button; press the button again to unmute the sound.

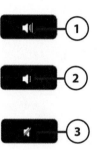

Chrome OS
desktop

Toshiba Chromebook 2

In this chapter, you'll learn how to turn your Chromebook on and off, how to navigate the desktop, and how to enter and emerge from sleep mode.

→ Starting Up and Shutting Down
→ Navigating the Chrome OS Desktop
→ Navigating Windows and Tabs

Using Chrome OS and the Chrome Desktop

Using a Chromebook is similar to using a traditional notebook computer, but faster. Because less operating system overhead is involved, as well as fewer internal components, a Chromebook boots up much quicker than a Windows or Mac machine; it wakes up from sleep mode almost immediately.

What you find after you start up your Chromebook, however, may not be totally familiar to you, especially if you're used to using a Windows or Mac notebook. To use your Chromebook, you need to get used to the Chrome OS interface.

Starting Up and Shutting Down

The most basic computer operations are turning the computer on and turning it off. Your Chromebook should start up in less than 10 seconds, and power down almost immediately.

Start Up and Log In

Your Chromebook can be run either on battery power or connected to an external AC power source. Once it powers up, you then have to log in to the computer with your username and password.

1. To power up your Chromebook, simply open the case and lift the LCD display panel.

   Or

2. If the LCD panel is already opened, press the Power button.

Power Button

The small LCD on the Power button lights when your Chromebook is turned on.

3. When the login screen appears, select your user account (if you have more than one account on this machine) and enter your password.

4. Press Enter.

Google Chrome now launches and displays the desktop.

Put Your Chromebook to Sleep

Although you can completely power off your Chromebook, you may prefer to enter sleep mode instead. This is good for when you're not actively using the Chromebook for a period of time, but expect to resume use soon; it conserves your Chromebook's battery life.

The advantage of sleep mode over powering down your Chromebook is that when you're ready to resume use, your Chromebook will resume operation immediately. If you instead opt to power down and then restart your Chromebook, you'll have to sit through the (admittedly short) startup process and then reenter your password.

Screensaver

Your Chromebook will automatically turn off its screen after six minutes of inactivity (eight minutes if you're using external power). You redisplay the screen by swiping across the touchpad or pressing any key on the keyboard.

1. To enter sleep mode, close the lid of your Chromebook.

2. To wake up from sleep mode, open the lid of your Chromebook.

Power Off Your Chromebook

Shutting off your Chromebook is a simple matter of pressing the Power button. Unlike other operating systems, Chrome OS does not require a menu operation to power off.

1. Press and hold the Power button for 2 seconds. The screen shrinks and, if you release the button now, Chrome goes into screen lock mode.

2. Continue holding the Power button for an additional 2 seconds.

Your Chromebook now completely powers off. You can restart your Chromebook by following the start-up procedure previously described.

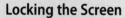

Locking the Screen

Chrome OS features a screen lock mode that displays the Chrome login screen. To access screen lock mode, press and hold the Power button for 2 seconds and then release the Power button. To resume normal operation, select your username, enter your password, and then press Enter. To power off from screen lock mode, simply close the Chromebook's lid.

It's Not All Good

If for some reason your Chromebook freezes or refuses to shut down normally, you can force a shutdown by pressing and holding the Power button for at least 8 seconds.

Navigating the Chrome OS Desktop

Chrome OS features a desktop interface that looks and feels similar to the Windows or Mac OS desktop. You can open multiple windows to appear on the desktop, and size and arrange those windows as you like.

Desktop

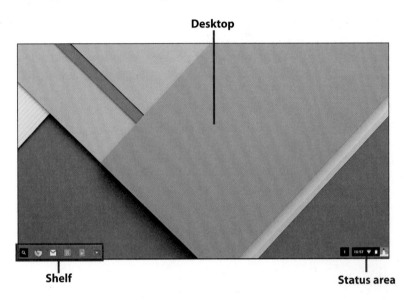

Shelf   **Status area**

>>>*Go Further*

AUTOHIDE THE SHELF

By default, the Shelf and status area always appear at the bottom of the desktop screen. If you want a little more screen room, you can configure the Shelf to automatically hide until you move your cursor to the bottom of the screen.

To autohide the Shelf (and status area), right-click at the bottom of the screen and then check Autohide Shelf. To deactivate the autohide feature, right-click the bottom of the screen and uncheck Autohide Shelf.

Shelf and Launcher

At the bottom left of the desktop is the Shelf, which is kind of like the taskbar in Windows. This area contains icons for your most popular applications. By default, the Shelf hosts icons for the Launcher, Google Chrome, Gmail, Google Search, Google Docs, and YouTube; you can also pin other apps to the Shelf. Click an icon to launch that app in a new window.

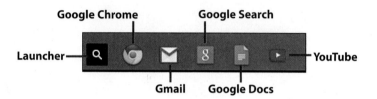

Google Chrome   **Google Search**

Launcher   **YouTube**

Gmail   **Google Docs**

The first icon in the Shelf is the Launcher. When you click the Launcher icon, Chrome displays the Launcher panel. This panel includes icons for your most recently used apps, as well as an All Apps icon.

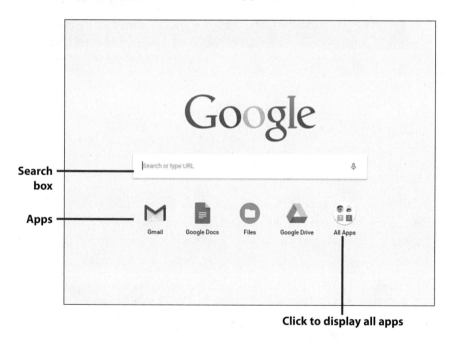

Search box

Apps

Gmail   Google Docs   Files   Google Drive   All Apps

Click to display all apps

Click the All Apps icon in the Launcher panel to display the Apps panel, which displays icons for all the apps installed on your Chromebook, arranged in multiple tabs. You can add more apps to your Chromebook by visiting the Chrome Web Store.

Apps

Tabs

You can also search your apps and favorite websites from either the Launcher or All Apps panel. Just enter your query into the Search box at the top and then press Enter. Chrome will now display a list of matching apps and web pages you've visited.

Chrome Web Store

Learn more about Chrome apps and the Chrome Web Store in Chapter 10, "Using Chrome Apps and Extensions."

>>>Go Further

MOVE THE SHELF

By default, the Shelf appears at the bottom of the screen. You can, however, move the Shelf to either side of the screen, where it appears vertically. To move the Shelf, right-click at the bottom of the screen, click Shelf Position, and then select Left, Bottom, or Right.

Status Area

At the bottom right of the Chrome desktop is the status area. This area includes information about your system and access to your personal settings.

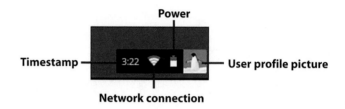

The three main status icons in the status area are Timestamp, Network Connection, and Power. A fourth icon displays the profile picture for the currently signed-in user.

The following table details the icons you might encounter in the status area.

Chrome OS Status Icons

Icon	Status Type	Description
4:28	Timestamp	Displays current time.
	Network Connection	Connected to a non-secure Wi-Fi network. The number of "lit" signal bars indicates the strength of your connection.
	Network Connection	Connected to a secure Wi-Fi network.
	Network Connection	No Wi-Fi connection.
	Network Connection	Connected to a wired network.
	Network Connection	Connected to a wired network; no network connection.
	Power	Operating on battery power. The amount of battery time left is indicated by the "fill" level of the battery icon.
	Power	Operating on external power; recharging battery.

Click anywhere in the status area to display the Settings panel. You can do the following from this panel:

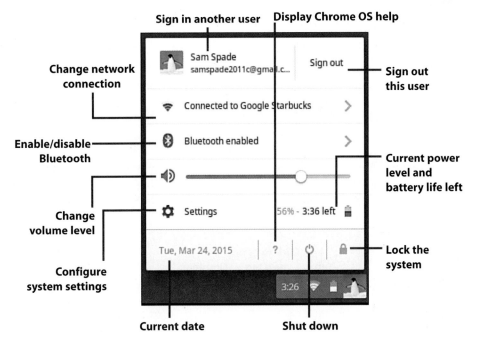

- Switch to another account, by clicking your username.

- Sign out of the current account, by clicking Sign Out.

- Change your network connection, by clicking Connected To.

- Enable or disable external Bluetooth devices, by clicking Bluetooth.

- Raise or lower your Chromebook's volume level, by using the speaker control.

- Configure additional Chrome OS settings, by clicking Settings.

- Display Chrome's help system, by clicking the question mark (?) icon.

- Shut down your Chromebook, by clicking the power icon.

- Lock your system (requires your password to resume normal operation), by clicking the lock icon.

Chrome OS Settings

Learn more about configuring the Chrome OS settings in Chapter 6, "Configuring and Personalizing Chrome OS."

Navigating Windows and Tabs

Every app you open in Chrome appears in a Chrome browser window. This window is much like the Chrome web browser available for both the Windows and Mac operating systems. Different apps appear in different tabs within the main window; you can also remove tabs from the browser to create multiple browser windows on the desktop.

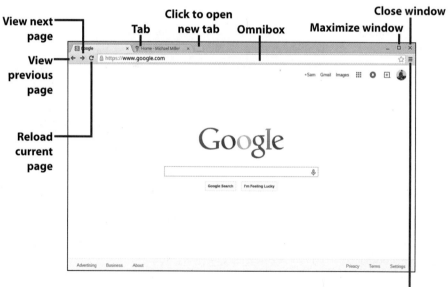

Customize and Control button

Along the top of the Chrome browser are all your open tabs, as well as a small blank tab that you use to open additional tabs. Below the row of tabs and indicators is Chrome's Omnibox. This is where you enter web page URLs or search queries. To the left of the Omnibox are buttons to switch to the previous and next pages viewed, and a Reload button for refreshing the current page.

To the right of the Omnibox is the Customize and Control Google Chrome button. Click this button to display a menu of system settings for the Chrome browser and your Google Account.

When you open a new tab, Chrome displays its default home page. This New Tab tab displays those web pages you've most recently visited. There are links at the bottom of the page to view web pages viewed on other devices attached to your Google Account, recently closed tabs, and the Google Chrome Web Store. This page also displays the Bookmarks bar, which includes all web pages that you've bookmarked.

Open a New Chrome Window

If no window is currently open, you can open a new window by clicking the Chrome icon on the Shelf.

If a window is currently open, there are two ways to open a new window:

- Click the Customize and Control button and then click New Window.
- Press Ctrl+N from the Chromebook keyboard.

Customize and Control button

New Window from Tab

You can drag any existing tab from the browser window to the Chrome desktop. This opens a new window for the page or app in that tab.

Open New Tabs

You have three ways to open a new tab in the current browser window:

- Click the Customize and Control button and then click New tab.
- Click the small blank tab at the end of the browser's tab row.
- Press Ctrl+T on the Chromebook keyboard.

Click to open new tab   Customize and Control button

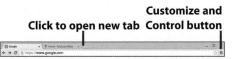

Navigate Tabs

Chrome can display multiple tabs, each displaying a different web page or running a specific web app.

1. To go directly to any open tab, click that tab.

2. To close a tab, click the X on that tab.

3. To switch to the next open tab, press Ctrl+Tab.

Manage Window Size

It's easy to change the size of any open window on the desktop.

1. To minimize a window to the Shelf, click the Minimize button.

2. To maximize a window, so that it appears full screen, click the Maximize button on the top-right corner of the window. Alternatively, press the Full Screen button on the Chromebook keyboard.

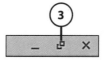

3. To return a maximized window to its previous size, click the Maximize button again.

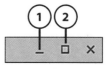

4. To dock a window to the left side of the screen, drag the window's title bar to the left side of the screen.

5. To dock a window to the right side of the screen, drag the window's title bar to the right side of the screen.

6. To resize a window, mouse over any window edge or corner until the cursor changes shape; then drag the cursor to resize the window.

Switch Between Open Windows

Chrome lets you open multiple windows, each with its own set of tabs, and then switch between windows. There are two ways to switch to the next open window in Chrome:

- Press the Next Window button on the top row of your Chromebook's keyboard.

- Press Alt+Tab on the Chromebook keyboard.

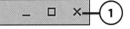
—Next Window button

Switching Tabs

To switch between tabs in an open browser window, press Ctrl+Tab.

Close the Window

Closing any open window is a one-click operation.

1. Click the X at the top right of the window.

User 1   User 2

In this chapter, you'll learn how to create multiple users for your Chromebook, how to switch from user to user, and how to use Chromebook's Guest account.

4

Managing Multiple Users

A Chromebook is only a piece of hardware; all of your personal settings, information, and data are stored on the Web. As such, you can log in to any Chromebook machine with your Google Account, and it will look and feel just like your own Chromebook. And it's easy enough for other users to log in to your Chromebook, as well, and make it their own.

How easy is it to add new users to a Chromebook? Pretty easy, as you'll soon discover.

Adding Users to Your Chromebook

When you first started up your Chromebook, you were prompted to enter your Google Account name and password. This account becomes your default user account on your Chromebook. You can, however, add other users to your Chromebook—that is, let other people with Google Accounts use this particular Chromebook.

Add a User

You can let any number of users log on to your Chromebook, as long as they all have Google Accounts.

1. Click the status area to display the Settings panel.

2. Click Sign Out.

3. From the login screen, click Add User.

4. When the Sign In screen appears, enter the new user's Gmail address into the Email field.

5. Enter the user's Gmail password into the Password field.

6. Click the Sign In button.

7. When the next screen appears, select a picture for your account.

8. Click the OK button.

Chrome now displays the Welcome to Your Chromebook window. Close this window to begin using Chrome as normal. The next time you open your Chromebook, this account will be one of the options on the login screen.

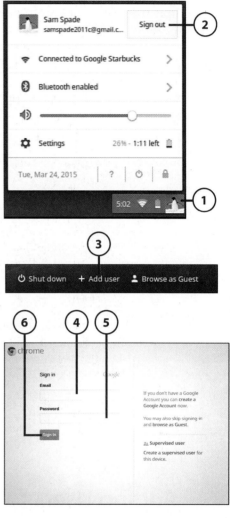

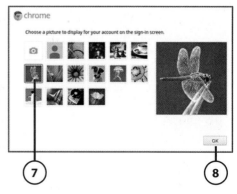

>>>Go Further
USING OTHER CHROMEBOOKS

With the Chrome OS, you're not limited to a single Chromebook. You can also use other people's Chromebooks by logging in to your Google Account on those machines.

When you log in to any Chromebook with your Google Account, that Chromebook displays all the apps and personalization you've made to your own Chromebook. In essence, your Chromebook settings travel from machine to machine; they're tied to your account in the cloud, not to any particular piece of hardware.

Add a Supervised User

In addition to normal users, you can also add *supervised users* to your Chromebook. With a supervised user, you can control and view the websites that person visits. It's perfect for the children in your household, who you don't want visiting inappropriate sites on the Web.

1. Click the status area to display the Settings panel.

2. Click Sign Out.

3. From the login screen, click Add User.

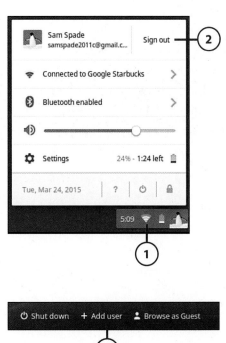

4. In the next panel, on the right side, click Create a Supervised User.

5. Read about supervised users, if you like, and then click the Create Supervised User button.

6. From the list of registered users, click the person you want to manage the new supervised account.

7. Enter the password for that user.

8. Click Next.

9. Enter a name for the new supervised user.

10. Enter the desired password for the new user into the Enter Password box; then re-enter it into the Confirm Password box.

11. Click to select a profile picture for the new user.

12. Click Next.

13. You now see the final screen, with information about the new user. Click the Got It! button to finish.

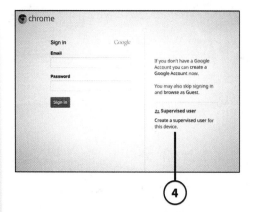

Control Sites Supervised Users Can Visit

After you create a new supervised user, it's your job to supervise that user's web browsing. You do this from the Supervised Users Dashboard, accessible from the Chrome browser at www.chrome.com/manage.

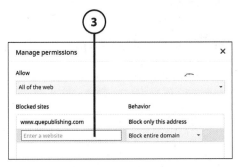

1. Select the user you want to manage from the list on the left.

2. In the Permissions box, click Manage to display the Manage Permissions panel.

3. By default, the supervised user has access to the entire Web. To block the user's access to a specific site, enter the site's URL into the Enter a Website box in the Blocked Sites section. Repeat this step to enter additional unapproved sites.

4. To allow access only to a list of approved sites, click the Allow control and select Only Approved sites.

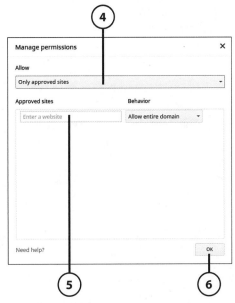

5. Enter a site you approve into the Enter a Website box in the Approved Sites section. Repeat this step to enter additional approved sites.

6. Click OK when finished.

7. To view a list of sites visited by the supervised user, scroll to the Activity section.

8. To see any requests from the supervised user to view a blocked site, scroll to the Requests section.

9. To approve a request, check the request and then click the Allow button.

10. To deny a request, check the request and then click the Deny button.

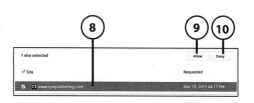

Editing User Information

Don't like the picture you've chosen for your Chromebook user account? It's easy enough to change—along with other information in your Google Account.

Change Your Profile Picture

Google Chrome lets you choose from a selection of built-in icons for your user account picture, upload an existing picture, or shoot a new picture using your webcam.

1. Click anywhere in the status area to display the Settings panel.

2. Click Settings.

3. When the Settings page appears, scroll to the People section and click the thumbnail image.

4. From the Change Picture panel, click one of the icons to use for your picture and then click Done.

5. To take a picture with your Chromebook's webcam and use it for your account picture, click the Camera icon. When the live image from your webcam appears, smile into the camera and click the green camera button. If you like the picture that results, click the OK button.

6. To upload a stored picture for your account picture, click the Folder icon. When the Select a File to Open panel appears, navigate to and select the file you want to upload and then click the Open button.

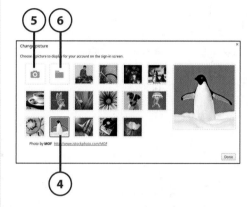

Edit Your Profile

Your Chromebook account is tied to your Google Account, in that they both use the same username (email address) and password. This lets you log in to your account from any Chromebook.

Your Google Account is used by all Google services and applications, and includes your personal account profile. If this is a new Google Account, you'll need to create a new profile. You can also edit your profile at any time.

1. Open a new Chrome window and go to www.google.com.

2. Click your account name or picture in the top-right corner of the page and select View Profile.

3. When your profile page appears, click the About tab.

4. Go to the section of your profile you want to edit and then click Edit for that section. This opens a panel for editing.

5. Enter the appropriate information for that section.

6. Click the Save button when you're done entering information for that section.

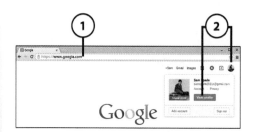

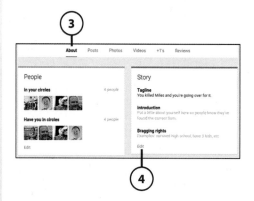

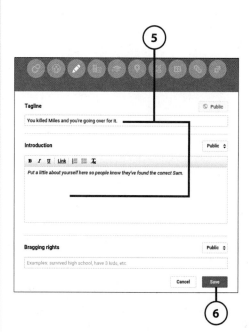

Google Account

A single Google Account provides your own personal access to all of Google's various sites and services. That includes personalized search results from Google's search engine (www.google.com), email service from Gmail (mail.google.com), online calendars on Google Calendar (www.google.com/calendar/), and your own account on Google+ (plus.google.com), Google's new social network.

Switching Users

If you've created multiple user accounts for your Chromebook, it's easy to switch from one user account to another—without shutting down your machine.

Switch User Accounts

To switch users, you need to sign out from one account on your Chromebook and sign in to another.

1. Click anywhere in the status area to display the Settings panel.

2. Click Sign Out.

3. Your Chromebook now displays the login screen. Select the user account to log in to, enter the password, and press Enter.

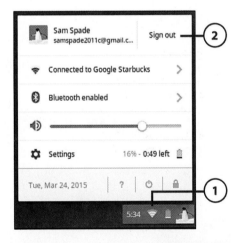

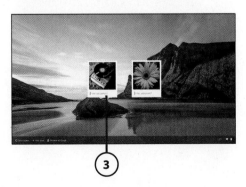

Log In as a Guest User

Any person can log in to your
Chromebook as a Guest user. A
Guest user has limited use of the
Chromebook; he or she can browse
the Web, but not save or access files
on your machine. In addition, a Guest
user's browsing and search history
are not saved.

1. Click anywhere in the status area
   to display the Settings panel.

2. Click Sign Out.

3. Your Chromebook now displays
   the log in screen. Click Browse
   as Guest.

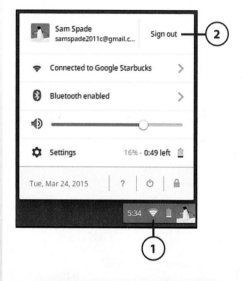

Wireless networks

In this chapter, you'll learn how to connect to and manage wireless networks for your Chromebook.

→ Connecting to a Wi-Fi Network
→ Connecting to an Ethernet Network
→ Managing Network Connections

5

Working Wirelessly

Chrome OS is a web-based operating system; to fully use your Chromebook, you must be connected to the Internet. All Chromebooks include built-in Wi-Fi wireless connectivity, so you can connect to the Internet over any nearby Wi-Fi network. And, despite the Chromebook being primarily a portable device, it's also possible to connect a Chromebook to a wired network to access the Internet. Which option you use depends on your own specific circumstances.

Connecting to a Wi-Fi Network

Most users will connect their Chromebooks to the Internet via some sort of Wi-Fi wireless connection. Wi-Fi is Chrome's default connection method, as most homes and offices are set up with Wi-Fi connectivity; also, numerous public Wi-Fi hotspots are available at coffee houses, hotels, restaurants, and the like.

Supported Networks

The current generation of Chromebooks can connect to 802.11 a/b/g/n Wi-Fi networks, using any of the following wireless security schemes: WEP, WPA-PSK, and WPA-Enterprise.

View Network Status

The Network icon in the status area at the bottom right of the Chrome desktop indicates the status of your Wi-Fi connection, as detailed in the following table.

Wi-Fi Status Icons

Icon	Status
	Connected to a Wi-Fi network
	No Wi-Fi connection

Enable Wi-Fi on Your Chromebook

Wi-Fi connectivity is enabled by default on most Chromebooks. If necessary, however, you can enable Wi-Fi manually.

1. Click anywhere in the status area to display the Settings panel.

2. Click No Network; the Settings panel changes and the message "Wi-Fi Is Turned Off" appears.

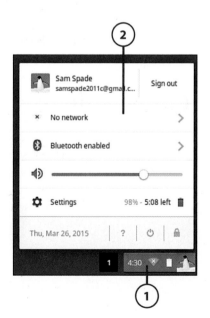

3. Click Turn Wi-Fi On. A list of available networks is displayed.

Disabling Wi-Fi

If Wi-Fi is enabled, you can disable Wi-Fi by opening the Settings panel and clicking the Wi-Fi icon.

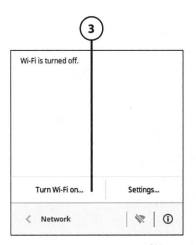

Connect to an Open Wi-Fi Network

Once Wi-Fi is enabled on your Chromebook, connecting to a Wi-Fi network is as easy as selecting the network from a list. Many Wi-Fi networks (especially public ones) are "open," in that anyone can connect without supplying a password.

1. Click anywhere in the status area to display the Settings panel.

2. Click No Network.

3. Chrome displays a list of nearby available wireless networks. Open networks are marked with a regular wireless icon; private networks (those that require passwords to access) have a lock next to the icon. Click the open network to which you want to connect.

The network name is now displayed with the word "Connecting" next to it. When "Connecting" disappears, you're connected.

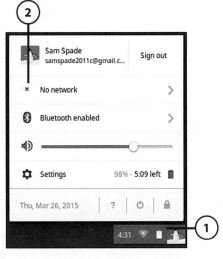

>>>Go Further
PUBLIC NETWORKS

Some public Wi-Fi networks, such as those you find in a coffee shop or hotel, may require additional login information after you've connected to the network. In most instances, a proprietary login screen will appear when you first attempt to view a website; you'll then need to follow the onscreen instructions to connect.

For example, when you connect to Starbucks' Wi-Fi, you first connect to the open Google Starbucks or ATTWIFI network. (Starbucks uses different Wi-Fi providers in different locations.) The first time you connect, you'll be prompted to log in to the network. Click this prompt to open the Chrome browser, with the network's log-in page displayed. Click the Accept and Connect button to accept Starbucks' terms and conditions and connect to the network.

In other instances, such as at some hotels, you may be asked to provide a password provided by the establishment when you first use your web browser. If the Wi-Fi service isn't free, you may also be asked to provide a credit card for billing, or okay billing to your room number.

Connect to a Secure Wi-Fi Network

Many Wi-Fi networks, especially home and business networks, are secure, in that they require a password for access. You'll need to supply this password to connect to a secure network.

1. Click anywhere in the status area to display the Settings panel.

2. Click No Network.

3. Chrome displays a list of nearby available wireless networks. Secure networks (those that require a password for access) are marked with a "locked" icon. Click the network to which you want to connect.

4. Chrome now displays the Join Wi-Fi Network dialog box; enter the password for the network.

5. Click the Connect button to connect.

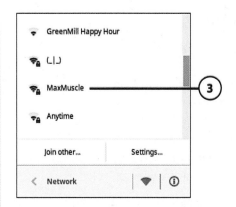

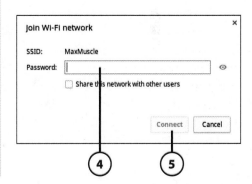

Connecting to an Ethernet Network

In some instances, you'll get better performance by making a wired connection to your network instead of a wireless one. An Ethernet connection is both faster and more stable than a Wi-Fi connection; it's also more secure, virtually immune to outside hacking.

Because the Chromebook is designed to be a wireless device, however, connecting via Ethernet is a secondary option. Although a handful of current-generation Chromebooks include Ethernet ports, most don't. If your Chromebook does not have an Ethernet port, you'll need to purchase an external USB Ethernet adapter, which plugs in to a USB port on your computer.

Connect via Ethernet

If your Chromebook has an Ethernet port, connecting to your network via Ethernet is as easy as connecting a cable.

1. Connect one end of an Ethernet cable to an Ethernet port on your Chromebook, or to a USB-to-Ethernet adapter.

2. Connect the other end of the Ethernet cable into your network router.

The Network icon in the status area changes to an Ethernet icon and indicates the status of your connection.

No Access

An "X" on the Ethernet icon indicates that you're physically connected to the network but do not have network access.

>>>Go Further
NO HOME NETWORKING

The Chromebook is designed as an Internet device; it is not a networking computer. Even though you connect to the Internet via a wireless network, you can't access other assets on the network.

This means you can't use your Chromebook to access other computers connected to the network, share files stored on the network, or access a network printer. For that matter, other network computers can't see or access your Chromebook, even when it's connected through a given network.

The only way to share files with other network users is to access those files via a cloud-based service, such as Google Drive, or email the files using Gmail.

Managing Network Connections

If you connect to the Internet in different locations, chances are you connect through a variety of different wireless networks. Managing your available wireless networks, then, is important.

Automatically Connect to a Network

If you have a favorite wireless network at a given location where multiple networks may be available, you can configure your Chromebook to automatically connect to your network of choice.

1. Make sure you're connected to the network in question; then click anywhere in the status area to display the Settings panel.

2. Click the network you're connected to. The panel changes.

3. Click the currently connected network to display a panel for that network.

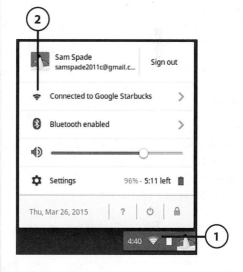

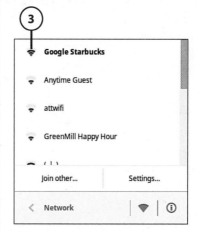

4. Check the Automatically Connect to This Network option.

5. Click the Close button.

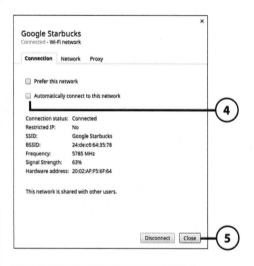

Forget a Network

Chrome automatically saves details about each and every network you connect to. If there is a network to which it's unlikely you'll ever connect again, you can clear the details for that network—in effect, you tell Chrome to forget that network.

1. Click anywhere in the status area to display the Settings panel.

2. Click Settings.

3. When the Settings page appears, go to the Internet Connection section, click the Wi-Fi Network menu, and select Preferred Networks.

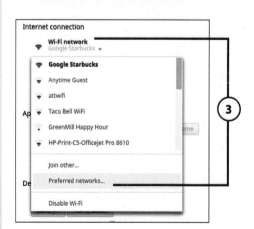

4. When the Preferred Networks dialog box appears, click the X next to the network you want to forget.

5. Click the Done button.

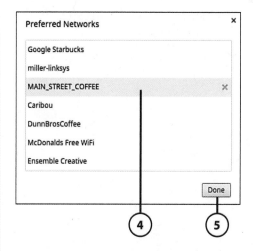

View Network Details

In some circumstances you may be asked to provide information about the wireless network to which you're connected. Chrome OS can display those details.

1. Make sure you're connected to the network in question; then click anywhere in the status area to display the Settings panel.

2. Click the network you're connected to. The panel changes.

3. Click the currently connected network to display a panel for that network.

4. Click the Connection tab to see all the information about this network.

>>>*Go Further*

CONNECTING TO A CORPORATE NETWORK VIA VPN

Many large companies provide access to their corporate networks via Virtual Private Network (VPN) technology. If you're using your Chromebook for work purposes, you can connect it to your company's VPN.

Click the status area to display the Settings panel and then select Settings. From the Settings page, go to the Internet Connection section, click Add Connection, and then select Add Private Network. When the Add Private Network panel appears, enter the appropriate information (provided by your company's IT department) for your company's VPN. Click Connect and proceed from there. (If your company requires you to install certificate files, you'll be prompted to do that after you click Connect; your company should provide you with the necessary files.)

Desktop backgrounds

In this chapter you'll learn about the many configuration options available with Chrome OS, from changing Chrome's startup behavior to selecting a new desktop background.

→ Personalizing the Desktop
→ Configuring the Chrome Browser
→ Configuring Other Settings

6

Configuring and Personalizing Chrome OS

Chrome OS works just fine in its default configuration, but there are a lot of things about Chrome you can configure to create a more uniquely personal user experience.

Personalizing the Desktop

The Chrome OS desktop can be customized in terms of colors and background images. It's a quick and easy way to personalize your own Chrome experience.

Change the Desktop Background

Most users like to select their own pictures for their computer desktops. It's no different with Chromebooks, which is why Chrome OS offers the option of personalized background images. You can select from images provided by Google, images uploaded from your computer, or plain colored backgrounds.

1. Click anywhere in the status area to display the Settings panel.

2. Click Settings.

3. Go to the Appearance section of the Settings page and click the Set Wallpaper button to open the Wallpaper window.

From the Desktop

You can also display the Wallpaper window by right-clicking anywhere on the open desktop and selecting Set Wallpaper.

---

4. Select a tab to display wallpapers of a given type—All, Landscape, Urban, Colors, Nature, or Custom.

5. Click the wallpaper you wish to use. This image is now downloaded to your computer and set as your desktop background.

6. To select a solid color background, select the Colors tab and then click the desired color.

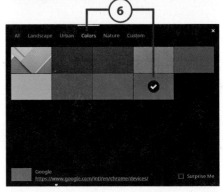

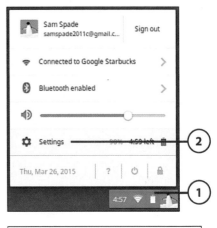

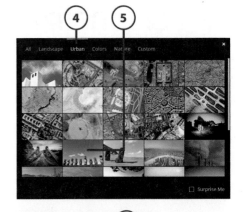

7. To upload your own personal image, select the Custom tab and then click the + tile.

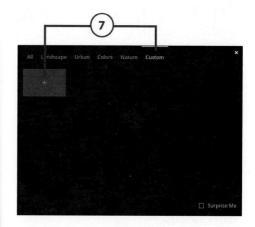

Surprise Me
To have your Chromebook display a random image on your desktop, check the Surprise Me option.

8. When the next pane appears, click the Choose File button to display the Select a File to Open window.

9. Navigate to and select the desired image file.

10. Click Open. You now see the image set as the desktop wallpaper.

11. If the image doesn't exactly fit the screen dimensions, click the Position button to determine how the image is displayed—Center, Center Cropped, or Stretch.

12. Click the X to close the panel.

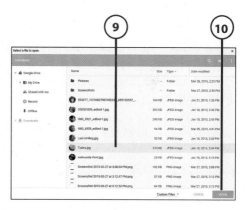

Configuring the Chrome Browser

Because the Chrome browser is where you do most of your work, you probably want to take a few minutes to configure the browser to your own personal preferences. You can change the home page displayed when the browser first launches, determine whether or not the Bookmarks bar is displayed, and change the entire look and feel of the browser by selecting a different theme.

Configure Startup Behavior

When you turn on your Chromebook and launch Chrome OS, one of three things can happen: Chrome can open the home page you set, reopen those pages that were open last, or open any pages you've preselected.

1. Click anywhere in the status area to display the Settings panel.

2. Click Settings.

Customize and Control
You can also open the Settings page by clicking the Customize and Control button at the top-right corner of the browser window.

3. Scroll to the bottom of the Settings page and click Show Advanced Settings.

4. To have Chrome open the default New Tab page on startup, scroll down to the On Startup section and select the Open the New Tab Page option.

5. To have Chrome open the pages that were last open on startup, scroll down to the On Startup section and select the Continue Where You Left Off option.

6. To have Chrome open pages you specify on startup, scroll down to the On Startup section and select the Open a Specific Page or Set of Pages option.

7. Click Set Pages to display the Startup Pages pane.

8. Enter the URL for the first page into the Add a New Page box. Press Enter to display an additional box, into which you can enter a second URL.

9. Continue adding URLs as desired; then click OK.

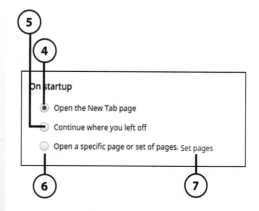

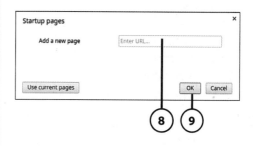

Use Current Pages

Another approach to specifying pages to open is to open the pages you want in separate browser tabs and then click the Use Current Pages button in the Startup Pages pane.

Display the Home Button

As you just learned, you can configure Chrome to open a specific home page on startup. You can also display a Home button in the toolbar, next to the Omnibox; clicking this Home button displays the page you've set as your home page.

1. Click anywhere in the status area to display the Settings panel.

2. Click Settings.

3. Go to the Appearance section of the Settings page and check the Show Home Button option.

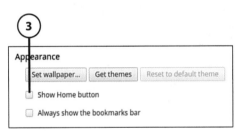

Display the Bookmarks Bar

Chrome lets you store bookmarks to your favorite pages on the Bookmarks bar. This is a toolbar that displays beneath the normal Chrome toolbar. You can then click a button on the Bookmarks bar to go directly to a bookmarked web page.

The Bookmarks bar displays automatically on the New Tab page. You can also opt to display the Bookmarks bar all the time in the Chrome browser.

1. Click anywhere in the status area to display the Settings panel.

2. Click Settings.

3. Go to the Appearance section of the Settings page and check the Always Show the Bookmarks Bar option.

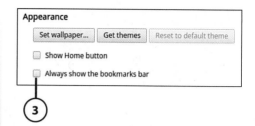

Alternate Method

Alternatively, you can click the Customize and Control button in the top-right corner of the Chrome browser and then click Bookmarks, Show Bookmarks Bar.

Change Search Providers

Chrome's Omnibox functions both as an address box and a search box. That is, you can enter a search query into the Omnibox and your query will be sent to your web search engine of choice.

Not surprisingly, Google is set as Chrome's default search engine provider. You can, however, opt to send your queries to any other search engine.

1. Click anywhere in the status area to display the Settings panel.

2. Click Settings.

3. Go to the Search section of the Settings page, click the first button (it should say "Google") and select a provider—AOL , Ask, Google, Yahoo!, or Bing.

4. To send your queries to a search engine not listed here, click the Manage Search Engines button.

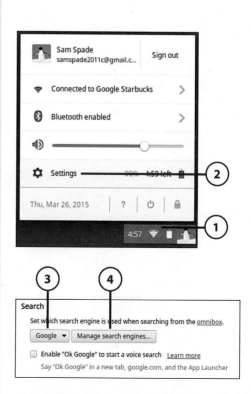

5. When the Search Engines panel appears, make a selection from the Other Search Engines section, or enter the name and URL of a different search engine.

6. Click Done.

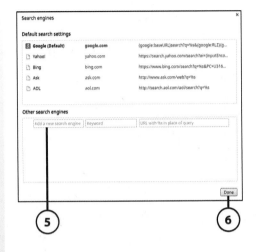

Enable Voice Search

When you're using Google's search engine, you don't have to type your queries. Instead, you can speak them and search via voice command. When this feature is activated, all you have to do is say "OK Google" into your Chromebook's microphone and then speak your query; Google will do the rest.

You will need to enable a feature called Google Instant. This feature, not enabled by default, displays predicted search results as you type your query.

1. Click anywhere in the status area to display the Settings panel.

2. Click Settings.

3. Go to the Search section of the Settings page and check the Enable "OK Google" to Start a Voice Search option.

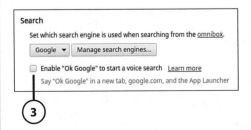

Select a New Theme

You can also change the look and feel of the Chrome browser window by selecting a new *theme*. A theme is a combination of colors, fonts, and background images; you can choose from any number of predesigned themes to personalize your browsing experience.

1. Click anywhere in the status area to display the Settings panel.

2. Click Settings.

3. Go to the Appearance section of the Settings page and click the Get Themes button. You are now connected to the Internet and taken to the Themes section of the Chrome Web Store.

4. Search for themes (using the Search the Store box in the left sidebar) or browse through all available themes.

5. Click a theme thumbnail to view information about that theme.

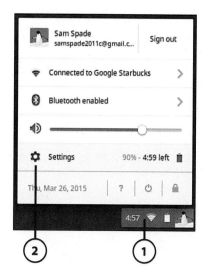

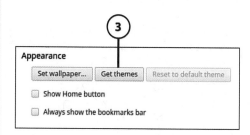

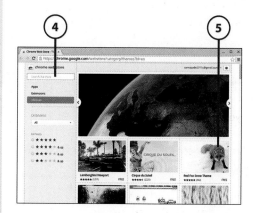

6. From the theme page, click the Add to Chrome button.

Reset to the Default Theme

You can return to Chrome's default theme at any time.

1. Click anywhere in the status area to display the Settings panel.

2. Click Settings.

3. Go to the Appearance section of the Settings page and click the Reset to Default Theme button.

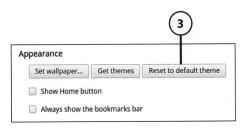

>>>*Go Further*
DIFFERENT THEMES

Some themes affect mainly the color of the Chrome browser window. For example, the Glow theme turns the tabs and frame black and puts a nice glow behind the tabs. The Gradient theme, on the other hand, paints the entire browser window in a cool blue gradient.

Other themes have more of a graphical element. For example, the Space Planet theme puts a ringed alien planet background in the browser window, whereas the Dale Chihuly theme turns the entire browser into a dazzling display of colorful blown glass, just like a display by the famous artist.

Configuring Other Settings

There's more you can customize about Google Chrome, all accessible from the Settings page—which you get to by clicking anywhere in the status area and then clicking Settings. (Some settings may only be visible when you click Show Advanced Settings at the bottom of the page.)

Configure the Touchpad

Don't like the way your Chromebook's touchpad works or feels? Then change it.

1. To change the sensitivity of the touchpad, go to the Device section and adjust the Touchpad Speed slider.

2. To disable tap-to-click functionality (which then requires you to tap only at the bottom area of the touchpad), click the Touchpad Settings button to display the Touchpad Settings panel.

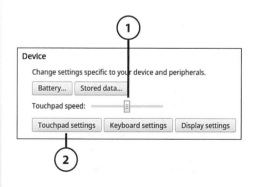

3. Uncheck the Enable Tap-to-Click option.

4. Click OK.

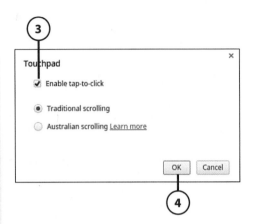

Change Search, Ctrl, and Alt Key Behavior

As previously noted, the Chromebook keyboard does not include some familiar keys, such as the Caps Lock key. You can, however, reconfigure how the Search, Ctrl, and Alt keys work in Chrome—and thus turn these keys into other keys that you might be missing.

Specifically, you can modify these keys as follows:

- **Search**—Change to Ctrl, Alt, Caps Lock, or disable.

- **Ctrl**—Change to Search, Alt, or disable.

- **Alt**—Change to Search, Ctrl, or disable.

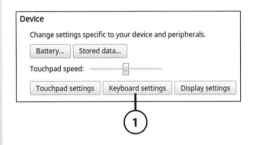

1. Go to the Device section and click the Keyboard Settings button.

2. When the Keyboard Settings panel appears, pull down the list for the key you wish to modify and make a new selection.

3. Click the OK button.

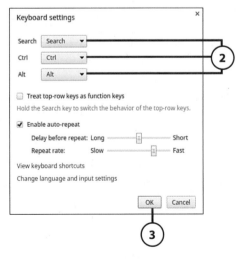

Wake from Sleep

If you want to keep strangers from accessing your Chromebook, you can require the entry of your user password whenever your device wakes from sleep mode. This is a nice bit of added security that ensures that nobody but you can access your running Chromebook and Google Account.

1. Scroll to the People section.

2. Check the Require Password to Wake from Sleep option.

Sync Your Account

Chrome OS and the Chrome browser are part of Google's Web-based cloud computing architecture. As such, if you use the Chrome browser on multiple computers (even Windows or Mac machines), you can configure Chrome to use the same bookmarks and settings on those other PCs.

Synchronization is enabled by default on your Chromebook. You can, however, configure just what settings you want to sync across all your computers.

Synchronization

This synchronization between devices is possible because Google saves all your bookmarks and settings online in your Google Account. Whenever or wherever you launch Chrome and connect to your Google Account, the settings you see will be the same ones you saved previously. Any changes you make from any computer are also saved online, and those changes are visible from other computers you use to access the Internet. So after you get your Chromebook properly configured, the Chrome browser will look and feel the same on any other computer you use.

1. Go to the People section and click the Advanced Sync Settings button.

2. Pull down the Sync Everything button and select either Sync Everything (default) or Choose What to Sync.

3. If you opted to choose what to sync, check any or all of the following items to synchronize: Apps, Autofill, Bookmarks, Extensions, History, Passwords, Settings, Themes & Wallpapers, and Open Tabs.

4. By default, Google automatically encrypts your account password for greater security. You can also opt to encrypt all the data synced in your Google Account by checking the Encrypt Synced Passwords with Your Google Credentials option.

5. Also by default, Google encrypts your passwords and data with your Google Account password. If you'd rather use a different password, select the Encrypt All Synced Data with Your Own Sync Passphrase option; then enter and confirm the new password.

6. Click the OK button.

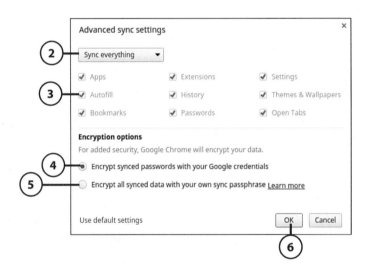

Disable Guest Browsing

Guest browsing is enabled by default in Chrome; this mode enables users not signed in to your computer to use it for basic tasks, such as browsing the Internet. If you'd rather not have unregistered users using your Chromebook, you can disable the guest browsing feature.

1. Go to the People section and click the Manage Other Users button.

2. Uncheck the Enable Guest Browsing box.

3. Click Done.

Owner-Only Settings

All settings that apply to other users of your Chromebook can only be configured by the machine's owner. If you are not the owner, you will see a message next to a red circle stating "These settings may only be modified by the owner."

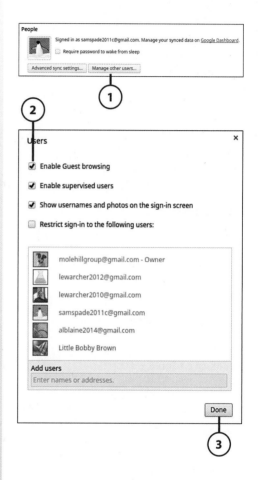

Hide Usernames

By default, you see the usernames and associated images for all users added to your Chromebook. You can, however, opt to hide these usernames and images.

1. Go to the People section and click the Manage Other Users button.

2. Uncheck the Show Usernames and Photos on the Sign-In Screen box.

3. Click Done.

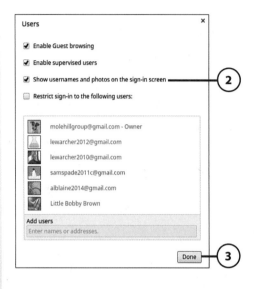

Restrict Sign-In

Another option is to restrict sign-in to a list of preapproved users. This way, only users you've okayed can sign in to your Chromebook.

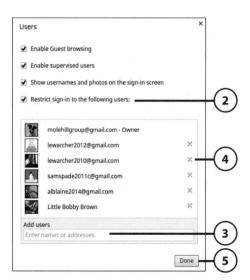

1. Go to the People section and click the Manage Other Users button.

2. Check the Restrict Sign-In to the Following Users option.

3. To add a user to the list, enter his or her username into the Add Users box and press Enter.

4. To delete a user from the approved list, click the X next to his or her name.

5. Click Done.

Change Your Time Zone

Chrome determines the current date and time over the Internet. However, it might not know your exact location—especially when you're traveling. Fortunately, it's easy to change the time zone displayed in Chrome.

1. Go to the Date and Time section, pull down the Time Zone list, and select your current time zone.

2. By default, Chrome uses a standard AM/PM clock. If you'd rather use a 24-hour military clock, check the Use 24-Hour Clock box.

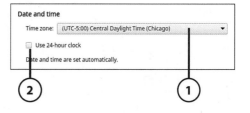

Configure Privacy Options

Privacy and security are important when you're browsing the Web. To that end, Chrome includes a variety of privacy-related settings in the Privacy section of the Settings page. We discuss these settings in Chapter 19, "Optimizing and Troubleshooting Your Chromebook." Turn there for more details.

Connect a Bluetooth Device

Many Chromebooks include built-in Bluetooth wireless, which is used to connect some wireless mice and keyboards. To connect an external Bluetooth device to your Chromebook, you first have to enable your device's Bluetooth functionality.

1. Go to the Bluetooth section and check the Enable Bluetooth option to expand the section.

2. To connect a Bluetooth device, click the Add a Device button to open the Add Bluetooth Device panel.

3. Your Chromebook begins searching for nearby Bluetooth devices. When the new device is found, highlight it in the list.

4. Click the Connect button.

5. Follow the onscreen instructions to connect your Bluetooth device. You may be prompted to enter a PIN for the connected device.

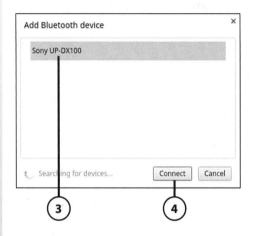

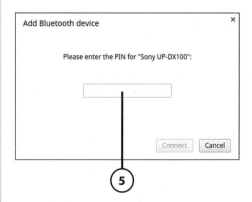

It's Not All Good

Bluetooth—or Not

If your Chromebook includes Bluetooth functionality, you'll see the Enable Bluetooth option on the Settings page. If the Enable Bluetooth option isn't there, your Chromebook doesn't have built-in Bluetooth.

Enable Autofill

If you do a lot of online shopping, you probably find yourself re-entering the same personal information on multiple shopping sites. You can simplify all this form entering by enabling Chrome's Autofill feature, which stores your basic information and enters it automatically whenever you encounter a similar form on a web page.

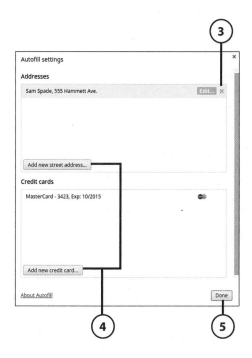

1. Go to the Passwords and Forms section and check the Enable Autofill… option.

2. To view and manage your AutoFill settings, click Manage Autofill Settings. The Autofill Settings panel displays with your saved addresses and credit cards.

3. To delete an item, mouse over it and click the X button.

4. To add a new item, click either the Add New Street Address or Add New Credit Card button.

5. Click Done.

Save Passwords

By default, Chrome will offer to save any passwords you enter when visiting web pages. This makes revisiting these pages that much faster and easier; Google enters the passwords for you, rather than your having to manually enter them yourself.

You can opt, however, for Google not to offer to save these passwords. This means you'll always have to enter required passwords manually—which makes for better security.

1. Go to the Passwords and Forms section and uncheck the Offer to Save Your Web Passwords option.

2. To delete any saved passwords, click Manage Passwords.

3. Sites where you've saved passwords appear at the top of the Passwords panel; sites where you've opted not to save passwords appear at the bottom. Mouse over a site in the Saved Passwords section and click the X to delete that password from the list.

4. To change a password for a given site, click the site and enter a new password into the box.

5. Click Done.

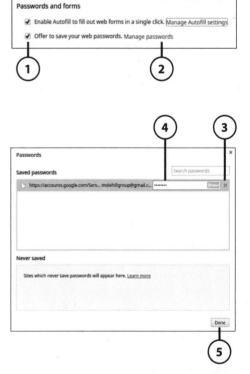

Display Web Content

Chrome offers several options that determine how web pages are displayed in the browser. In particular, you can change the size and type of fonts used, as well as change the zoom level when viewing pages.

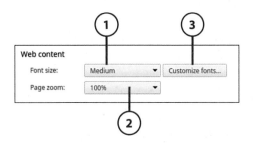

1. To change the size of the fonts used to display web pages, go to the Web Content section, pull down the Font Size list, and make a new selection from Very Small to Very Large. (Medium is the default size.)

2. To change the zoom level of the pages displayed, go to the Web Content section, pull down the Page Zoom list, and make a new selection.

3. To change the fonts used to display web pages, go to the Web Content section and click the Customize Fonts button.

4. To change the basic font, pull down the Standard Font list, make a new selection, and then adjust the slider to select the font size (from Tiny to Huge).

5. To change the serif font used, pull down the Serif Font list and make a new selection.

6. To change the sans serif font used, pull down the Sans-Serif Font list and make a new selection.

7. To change the fixed-width font used, pull down the Fixed-Width Font list and make a new selection.

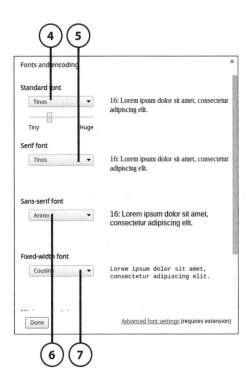

8. To change the smallest size font displayed, adjust the Minimum Font Size slider.

9. Click the Done button.

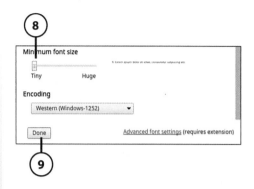

Customize Languages and Input Methods

By default, Chromebooks shipped in the U.S. display all menus and dialog boxes in English. If you speak another language, however, you can change this, and have Chrome display in a more familiar language.

You can also change the input method used for your Chromebook's keyboard. By default, Chrome uses a standard U.S. keyboard. You can opt instead to have your Chromebook mimic an international keyboard, extended keyboard, Dvorak keyboard, or Colemak keyboard.

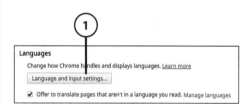

1. Go to the Languages section and click the Language and Input Settings button.

2. Click the Add button in the Languages section to add another display language. When the next dialog box appears, click the language you wish to use.

3. To change the keyboard input method, select another option from the Input Method section.

4. Click the Done button.

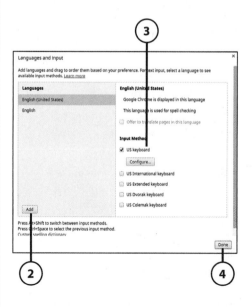

Translate Pages

If you often run across web pages from other countries, and you don't know the language, you can configure Chrome to automatically translate foreign pages.

1. Go to the Languages section.

2. Check the Offer to Translate Pages That Aren't in a Language You Read option.

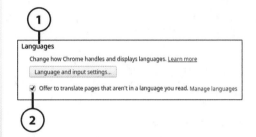

Manage Downloads

When you download files from the Web, those files have to be stored somewhere. By default, that location is the Downloads folder—although that's something you can customize.

1. Go to the Downloads section and click the Change button; then select a new folder.

2. If you want to be prompted for a new download location for each file, check the Ask Where to Save Each File Before Downloading option.

Disable Google Drive

Google Drive, Google's online storage service, shows up as a storage option when you're managing files on your Chromebook. You can, however, reconfigure Chrome so that you don't see Google Drive as an option.

1. Go to the Downloads section.

2. Check the Disable Google Drive on This Device option.

Manage Cloud Print

The Google Chrome OS does not enable printing directly from your Chromebook. Instead, you use Google's Cloud Print service to print to a printer connected to another computer. To learn more about configuring and using Cloud Print, turn to Chapter 18, "Printing with Google Cloud Print."

Enable Accessibility Features

If you have vision problems, using any operating system or web browser is difficult. Fortunately, Chrome includes several accessibility features that help you to find your way around the Chrome interface, all available in the Accessibility section of the Settings page.

1. To display a menu of accessibility options on the Settings panel (when you click in the status area), check Show Accessibility Options in the System Menu.

2. To display a larger mouse cursor for enhanced visibility, check Show Large Mouse Cursor.

3. To display the desktop and web page content with white type on a black background, check Use High Contrast Mode.

4. To enable the ability for keyboard shortcuts to be pressed sequentially (that is, if you press Shift or Ctrl, that key stays pressed until you press the next key in the shortcut), check Enable Sticky Keys.

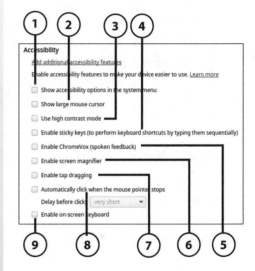

5. To enable spoken feedback for user actions, check Enable ChromeVox.

6. To enlarge the screen so that smaller elements are easier to see, check Enable Screen Magnifier.

7. To drag onscreen objects using one finger on the touchpad, check Enable Tap Dragging.

8. To automatically click "enter" when the cursor stops moving, check Automatically Click When the Mouse Pointer Stops. Click the Delay Before Click button to set the delay, from Extremely Short to Very Long.

9. To display the onscreen keyboard (useful on Chromebooks with touchscreens), check Enable On-Screen Keyboard.

>>>Go Further
CHROMEVOX

One of the most important accessibility features, especially for those with eyesight problems, is the ability to make the operating system speak to you. To enable this useful function, Google's ChromeVox screen reader provides spoken feedback for all user actions. When ChromeVox is activated, all of Chrome's menus talk, and opening a web page produces a combination of spoken feedback and auditory cues. ChromeVox also includes a set of keyboard commands you can use to navigate Chrome menus and web pages. To learn more about the ChromeVox screen reader, go to www.chromevox.com.

Reset to Default Settings

After you changed some of Chrome's settings, you may want to revert back to the original settings. You can do this with the click of a button.

1. Scroll to the Reset Settings section at the bottom of the Settings page.

2. Click the Reset Settings button.

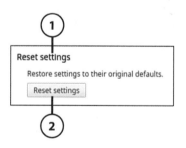

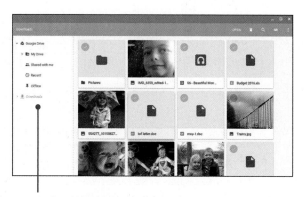

Chrome OS Files app

In this chapter, you learn how to manage stored and downloaded files on your Chromebook, and on external devices connected to your Chromebook.

→ Using the Files App
→ Using External Storage Devices

7

Managing Files and Using External Storage

Your Chromebook is designed to be a cloud-based computing device. That is, it's designed to work with web-based applications and files stored on the Web. As such, most Chromebooks don't have much in the way of internal storage—a relatively meager 16GB of flash memory (32GB on some more expensive machines) and no hard drive.

Although this is enough storage to hold the Chrome OS and a minimal number of pictures or other files you want to store locally, if you need additional storage space, you can connect USB memory devices and even external hard drives to your Chromebook. You manage all your local files using Chrome's built-in Files app. (And, of course, you can store anything you want online at Google Drive— which we'll cover in the next chapter.)

Using the Files App

The Files app in Chrome OS is similar in concept to the file management utilities found in the Windows and Mac operating systems. You can use the Files app to view, open, copy, cut, paste, and delete files stored in your Chromebook's memory and on external devices connected to your Chromebook. It's relatively easy to access and, because of its limited functionality, quite easy to use.

To open the Files app, press Alt+Shift+M on your Chromebook keyboard. You can also open the Files app by clicking the Launcher in the desktop Shelf, clicking All Apps, and then clicking the Files icon.

The Files app consists of two sections. The sidebar, on the left, displays the three main types of storage on your Chromebook: Google Drive (online storage with Google), Downloads (storage on the Chromebook itself), and any external devices you have connected. The main part of the Files window displays the contents of the selected storage or folder. There's a toolbar at the top, with controls relevant to the current selection.

The main window can display contents either as a list or as large thumbnails. You select the file view by clicking either the List View or Thumbnail View button at the top right of the Files window.

In List View, the contents of the selected folder are displayed by default in reverse chronological order—that is, the most recent files first. For each file, you see the file name, size, type, and date modified. You can sort by any of these attributes by clicking the top of the selected column.

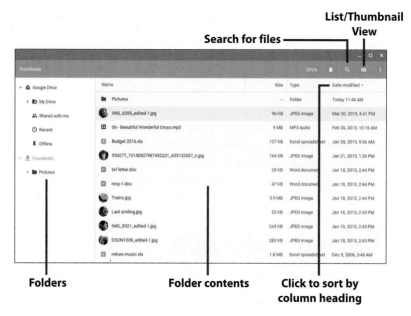

List/Thumbnail View

Search for files

Folders   **Folder contents**   **Click to sort by column heading**

In Thumbnail View, you see only the name of the file—along with a thumbnail image of the file's contents. For a picture file, the thumbnail is the picture itself. For other types of files, the thumbnail image is more generic, and sometimes reflective of the file type.

Delete selected file

Selected file   Open selected file

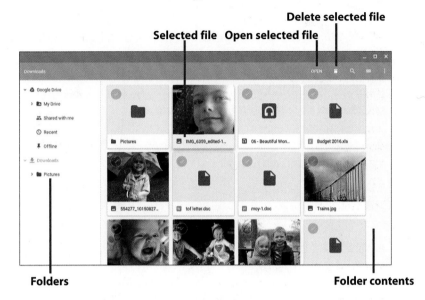

Folders   **Folder contents**

On the left side of the toolbar at the top of the Files app is a "bread crumb" list of all the folders and subfolders in the path above the current folder. Click any folder or subfolder in this list to return directly to that folder.

Folders and subfolders bread crumbs

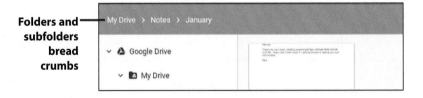

>>>Go Further

SUPPORTED FILE TYPES

Chrome can recognize many types of files, but not all. The following file types are officially recognized and supported by the Chrome OS:

- .bmp image files

- .doc and .docx Microsoft Word files (read-only)

- .gif image files

- .htm and .html web page files

- .jpg and .jpeg image files

- .mov video files

- .mp3 and .m4a audio files

- .mp4 and .m4v video files

- .ogv, .ogm, .ogg, and .oga Ogg Vorbis audio and video files

- .pdf Adobe Acrobat files

- .png image files

- .ppt and .pptx Microsoft PowerPoint files (read-only)

- .txt text files

- .wav audio files

- .webm video files

- .webp image files

- .xls and .xlsx Microsoft Excel files (read-only)

- .zip, .rar, .tar, .tar.gz, and .tar.bz2 compressed files

You can store other file types on your Chromebook, or on external devices connected to your Chromebook, but you cannot open, view, or play other file types within Chrome.

Open Files and Folders

You have several ways to open files and folders from within the Files app.

- Click the file or folder and then click Open in the toolbar.

- Double-click the file or folder.

- Right-click the file or folder and then select Open.

Right-click a file or folder and select Open

Double-click a file or folder

Select a file or folder and click Open

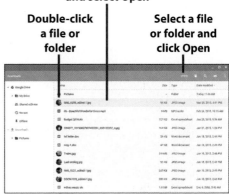

Rename Files and Folders

You can, if you wish, change the names of files from within the Files app.

1. From within the Files app, navigate to and right-click the file or folder you wish to rename.

2. Select Rename from the pop-up menu.

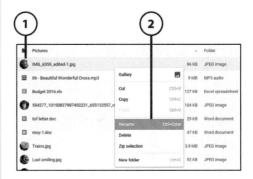

Right-Clicking

To right-click using your Chromebook's touchpad, press the touchpad with two fingers.

3. The file or folder name is now highlighted. Type the new name into the highlighted area and press Enter.

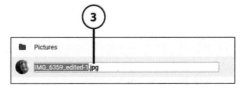

Copy a File

It's relatively easy to copy a file from its current location to another folder on your Chromebook, to an external storage device, or to your Google Drive.

1. From within the Files app, navigate to and right-click the file you want to copy.

2. Select Copy from the pop-up menu.

3. Navigate to and open the location where you wish to copy the file.

4. Right-click an open area of the Files window to display the pop-up menu and then click Paste.

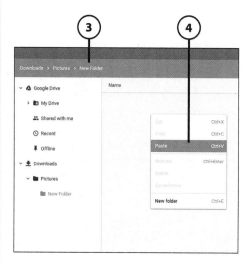

Move a File

Moving a file is different from copying it. When you copy a file, you leave the original file in its original location, and paste a copy of that file to a new location; two files remain. When you move a file, via the cut-and-paste operation, the file is removed from its original location and pasted into the new location; only one file remains.

1. From within the Files app, navigate to and right-click the file you want to move.

2. Select Cut from the pop-up menu.

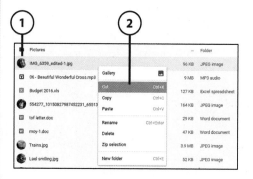

3. Navigate to and open the location where you wish to move the file.

4. Right-click an open area of the Files window to display the pop-up menu and then click Paste.

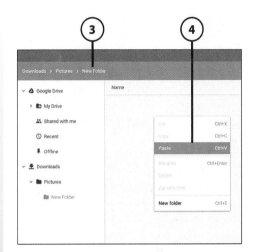

Delete Files

Naturally, the Files app lets you delete files and folders. This is often necessary to free up the limited storage space on your Chromebook.

1. Navigate to and click the file(s) or folder(s) you wish to delete.

Selecting Multiple Files

You can select multiple files from within the Files app. Just check the box for each file you wish to select, or hold down the Ctrl key while selecting multiple files.

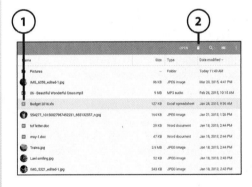

2. Click Delete in the toolbar. Alternatively, you can right-click and select Delete from the pop-up menu.

Create a New Folder

To better organize your stored files, you can use the Files app to create multiple folders and subfolders.

1. Navigate to the folder where you wish to add the new subfolder.

2. Right-click anywhere in an open area of the Files window to display the pop-up menu; then click New Folder.

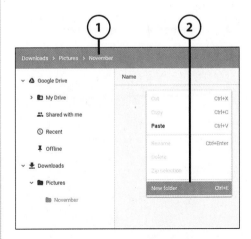

3. The Files app creates the new folder with the name area open for editing. Enter a name for the new folder and press Enter.

Save Files from the Web

Often, you'll find images and other files on websites that you'd like to save copies of. You can save these files directly to your Chromebook, or to a memory card or external USB memory device connected to your Chromebook.

Limited Storage

Because your Chromebook has limited storage on board, you should probably save most down-loaded files to an external storage device, or to your Google Drive.

1. From within the Chrome browser, right-click the file or image you want to save and then select Save Image As or Save File As from the pop-up menu.

2. When the Save File As window appears, select a folder in which to save the file.

3. Confirm or change the name of the file in the File Name field.

4. Click the Save button.

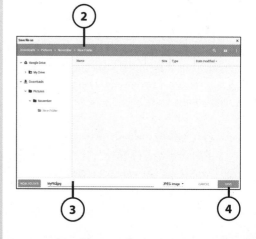

5. Chrome now displays the Downloads pane at the bottom of the browser window, with a button for the selected file on the far left. To view the downloaded file, click the file button.

6. To view all recently downloaded files, click the Show All Downloads link.

7. To close the downloads pane, click the X at the far right.

Using External Storage Devices

You can connect various types of external file storage to your Chromebook. In particular, you can connect USB memory devices, memory cards (such as those used in digital cameras), and any external hard drive that connects via USB.

Connect a USB Memory Device

You can connect any USB memory device (sometimes called a flash drive or thumb drive) to your Chromebook's USB ports and then access data stored on the drive using the Files app.

1. Insert the USB memory device into an open USB port on your Chromebook.

2. Chrome recognizes the USB device, and displays the message "Removable Device Detected." Within this message, click Open Files App.

Removable device detected
Explore the device's content in the Files app.

Open Files app

0   1:33

3. The Files app now opens, with the USB drive selected. Navigate within this device to find the file(s) you want.

(3)

It's Not All Good

Ejecting an External Storage Device

While you can simply remove an external storage device when you're done with it, Chrome doesn't always like this—and sometimes scolds you about it!. The better approach is to click the triangle icon next to the device's name in the Files app; this "ejects" or disconnects the drive, which you can then safely remove by hand.

Insert a Memory Card

The memory card slot found on most Chromebooks can read and write data to and from popular types of memory cards. These memory cards are typically used to store images taken from digital cameras. When you insert a memory card into your Chromebook, you can then view the images stored on the card. You can also use memory cards to store files downloaded from the Internet.

1. Insert the memory card into the memory card slot on your Chromebook.

(1)

2. Chrome recognizes the memory card, and displays the message "Removable Device Detected." Within this message, click Open Files App.

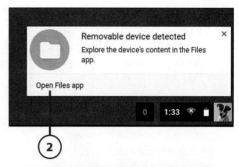

3. The Files app now opens, with the memory card selected. Navigate within this device to find the file(s) you want.

Screen Captures

If you need to capture a picture of the current screen on your Chromebook, press the Ctrl+Next Window button. Screen captures are stored in the Downloads folder.

Connect an External Hard Drive

Current-generation Chromebooks also let you connect external USB hard drives for additional storage. This way, you can store more and larger files than you can with the Chromebook's internal storage; you can also use the external hard drive to store backup copies of your most important files.

1. Connect one end of a USB cable to the USB connector on the external hard drive.

2. Connect the other end of the USB cable to an open USB port on your Chromebook.

3. Chrome recognizes the external drive, and displays the message "Removable Device Detected." Within this message, click Open Files App.

4. The Files app now opens, with the external drive selected. Navigate within this device to find the file(s) you want.

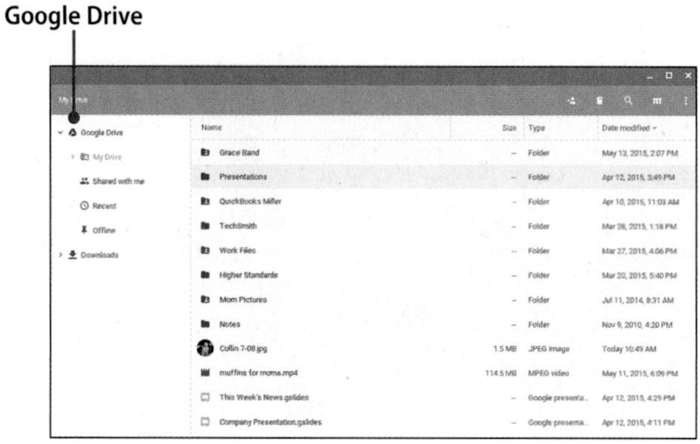
Google Drive
My Drive
Google Drive
My Drive
Shared with me
Recent
Offline
Downloads
Name
Size
Type
Date modified
Grace Band
Presentations
QuickBooks Miller
TechSmith
Work Files
Higher Standards
Mom Pictures
Notes
Collin 7-08.jpg
muffins for moms.mp4
This Week's News.gslides
Company Presentation.gslides

In this chapter, you learn how to store your important files on the Web using Google Drive.

→ Getting Started with Google Drive
→ Storing Files on Google Drive
→ Sharing with Google Drive

8

Using Google Drive to Store and Share Files

Chromebooks have minimal onboard storage space for files, no more than 32GB or 64GB in all, with many having 16GB. In fact, Chrome OS itself was built on the concept of cloud-based file storage.

With little local storage space available, then, where do you store your files? Online, of course. To that end, Google recommends its Google Drive cloud storage service. Google Drive makes it easy to access your important files from any computer, in any location. Google Drive is also great for sharing files with friends, family, and co-workers.

Getting Started with Google Drive

Google Drive appears as a storage device in your Chromebook's Files app. You can copy files to and from Google Drive as you would to and from any storage device or location.

Files App

Learn more about using Chrome's Files app in Chapter 7, "Managing Files and Using External Storage."

Configure Google Drive

As a Chromebook user, you get 100GB of free Google Drive storage for two years. That should be enough to hold all your important files, although additional storage is available for a fee. You set up your Google Drive account the first time you select Google Drive in the Files app.

1. Open the Chrome browser and go to **www.chromebook.com/goodies** to display the Google Drive welcome page.

2. Scroll to the Free 100 GB Storage with Google Drive section and click the Redeem Offer button.

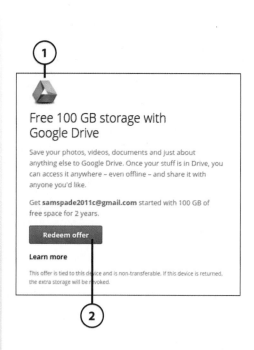

Free 100 GB storage with Google Drive

Save your photos, videos, documents and just about anything else to Google Drive. Once your stuff is in Drive, you can access it anywhere – even offline – and share it with anyone you'd like.

Get **samspade2011c@gmail.com** started with 100 GB of free space for 2 years.

Redeem offer

Learn more

This offer is tied to this device and is non-transferable. If this device is returned, the extra storage will be revoked.

Free Gogo Passes

For a limited time, you also get 12 free Gogo in-air Internet passes that you can use for the next two years on domestic U.S. flights. You redeem these passes from the same page where you redeem your 100GB Google Drive offer.

3. When prompted to verify that you're using an eligible Chrome OS device, click the Allow button.

4. Once your Chromebook is confirmed, click Start Using Google Drive. Google now displays the main Google Drive page (drive.google.com).

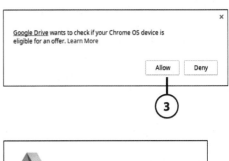

>>>Go Further

GOOGLE DRIVE STORAGE

By default, Google gives every Chromebook user 100GB of free Google Drive storage for two years. But other offers may be available, depending on which Chromebook model you purchase and when. For example, the Chromebook Pixel 2 comes with 1TB of free Google Drive storage for three years. As always, check with your Chromebook's manufacturer to see which offers are available.

If you need more storage space, you can purchase it from Google. An additional 100GB will cost you $1.99 per month; an additional 1TB of storage runs $9.99/month. Manage your Google Drive storage and purchase additional storage at www.google.com/settings/storage.

Storing Files on Google Drive

Although you can manage your Google Drive files from the Google Drive web page (drive.google.com), it's easier to do so from within Chrome's Files app.

View Your Google Drive Files

When you first sign up for Google Drive, you'll see a few "test" files in your main folder. You can delete these if you wish, and then begin using Google Drive to store additional files.

1. From within the Files app, go to the Google Drive section in the sidebar and click My Drive.

2. The contents of your main folder are now displayed; different types of files have their own distinctive icons. Click any subfolder to view those contents.

Copy a File to Google Drive

Copying a file from your Chromebook or external storage device to Google Drive is as easy as clicking and dragging.

1. From within the Files app, select the file you wish to copy to Google Drive.

2. Click and drag the file to the My Drive icon in the sidebar. The cursor changes to a thumbnail of the file while you're dragging it.

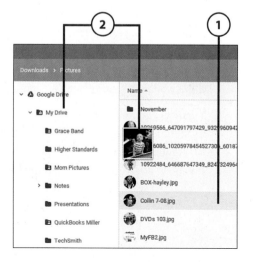

Copy and Paste

You can also copy a file to your Google Drive by right-clicking the file and selecting Copy; you then open your Google Drive folder, right-click, and select Paste.

Open a File from Google Drive

Opening a file stored on Google Drive is just like opening a file stored directly on your Chromebook.

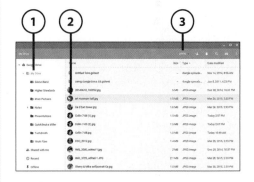

1. From within the Files app, click My Drive in the sidebar; then navigate to the file you wish to open.

2. Click to select the file you wish to open.

3. Click Open.

Delete Files from Google Drive

From time to time, it's good to free up space in your Google Drive folder by deleting old or unused files.

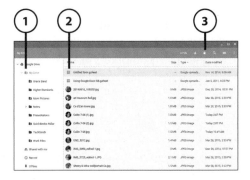

1. From within the Files app, click My Drive in the sidebar; then navigate to the file(s) you wish to delete.

2. Click to select the file(s) you wish to delete.

3. Click Delete in the toolbar. You will be asked if you are sure you want to delete the file. Click Delete.

Create a New Google Drive Folder

To better organize large numbers of files, you can create additional subfolders within your main Google Drive folder. You can then use these subfolders to store specific types of files. For example, you might create a subfolder just for work files or for holiday pictures.

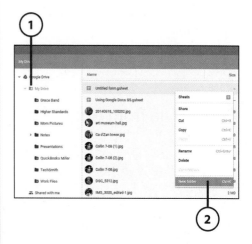

1. From within the Files app, click My Drive in the sidebar; then navigate to where you wish to create the new subfolder.

2. Right-click anywhere in an open area of the Files app window to display the pop-up menu; then click New Folder.

3. Google Drive creates the new folder with the name area open for editing. Enter a name for the new folder and press Enter.

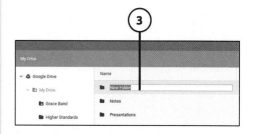

Sharing with Google Drive

Google Drive cloud storage is ideal for when you want to share a file with someone. Perhaps you want to share pictures with friends or family, or even collaborate on a group project for work. All you have to do is tell Google Drive to share that file with selected people, and then they can view it from their own computers or smartphone. (If you enable the proper access, they can edit the file, too.)

Share a File or Folder with Selected Users

You can also choose to share a file or folder with users you select. You can opt to let users only view or fully edit the given item.

1. From within the Files app, click My Drive in the sidebar; then navigate to the file or folder you wish to share.

2. Click to select the file or folder you wish to share.

3. Click the Share button to display the Share with Others pane.

4. By default, all your files are private, except for those you share with people you specify. To share the file with a person, enter his or her Google Account username or standard email address into the People box.

5. To make this file editable by the people you select, pull down the list to the right of the People box and select Can Edit.

6. To make this file read-only (that is, no one else but you can edit it), pull down the list to the right of the People box and select Can View.

7. Click the Done button. The selected person will now have access to the file—and receive an email (including a link to the file) inviting him or her to view it online.

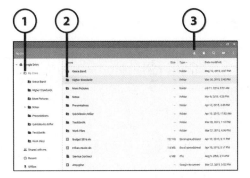

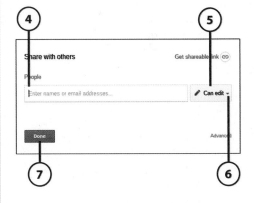

Share a Link to a File or Folder

Google Drive also lets you send a clickable link to anyone you wish to share the file with. You can copy and paste this link into email messages, Facebook posts, web pages, and the like.

1. From within the Files app, click My Drive in the sidebar; then navigate to the file or folder you wish to share.

2. Click to select the file or folder you wish to share.

3. Click the Share button to display the Share with Others pane.

4. Click Advanced to display the Sharing Settings pane.

5. By default, your Google Drive files and folders are not sharable in this fashion, so you need to change this setting. In the Who Has Access section, where it says Private, click Change.

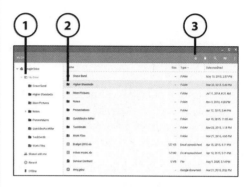

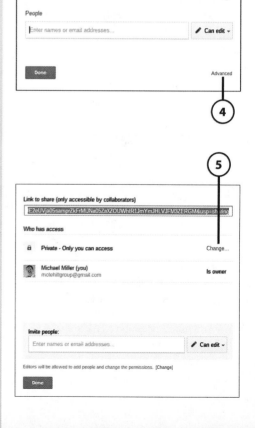

6. When the next pane appears, select On – Anyone with the Link.

7. In the Access: Anyone (No Sign-In Required) section, click the down arrow and select whether you want users to view (Can View) or edit (Can Edit) the item.

8. Click Save.

9. The link to this file or folder is displayed and highlighted. Right-click the link and select Copy.

10. Click Done to close the panel; then paste the link into the message, document, or post to send to other users.

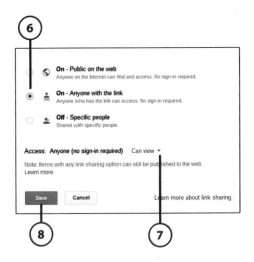

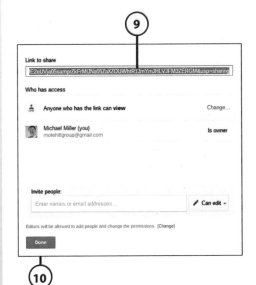

Chrome web browser

In this chapter, you learn how to use Google Chrome to browse and search the web.

→ Browsing the Web
→ Viewing and Managing Browser History
→ Searching the Web
→ Managing Your Home Page
→ Bookmarking Favorite Pages
→ Browsing in Incognito Mode

9

Browsing and Searching the Web

The Google Chrome OS is built around Google's Chrome web browser. Chrome (the browser) is similar to other web browsers available today, but with a sleeker interface—there's no menu bar, search bar, or status bar, as older browsers tend to have. This difference makes the web page bigger in the browser window, and simplifies the browsing experience. In essence, Chrome moves the business of the browser out of the way so that you can pay more attention to the web page itself.

Browsing the Web

Google's Chrome web browser is integrated into the Chrome OS interface. You use the Chrome browser to access all web-based apps, as well as most system settings.

The Chrome browser resembles Internet Explorer, Firefox, and other modern web browsers, complete with tabs for different web pages. To go to a web page, type the page's address (also called a URL) into the Omnibox at the top of the Chrome window; the web page then displays in the current tab.

Tab

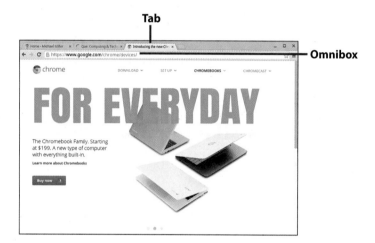

Omnibox

Omnibox

What other browsers call an Address box, Chrome calls the Omnibox. That's because it's more than a simple Address box; you can also use it to enter queries for web searches. When you start typing in the Omnibox, Google suggests both likely web pages and search queries. Just select what you want from the list or finish typing your URL or query; then press Enter.

Go to a Web Page

One of the quickest ways to browse the Web is to go directly to a given web page. You do this by entering the page's address, or URL, into Chrome's Omnibox.

1. Type a web page's URL into the Omnibox at the top of the Chrome window.

2. As you start typing in the Omnibox, Google suggests both queries and web pages you are likely to visit. Select the page you want from the drop-down list.

3. Alternatively, finish typing your URL and press Enter.

Chrome navigates to and displays the page you entered.

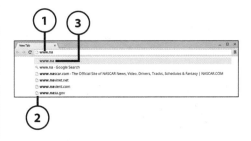

Click Links

Another way to navigate the Web is to click links to other pages you find on web pages. Clicking a link takes you directly to the linked-to page; you can open links in the current browser tab or, if you prefer to keep the current page visible, in a new tab or window.

- To open the link in the current tab, click the link.

- To open the link in a new tab, right-click the link and select Open Link in New Tab.

- To open the link in a new window, right-click the link and select Open Link in New Window.

Click a link   **Open Link in New Tab option**   **Open Link in New Window option**

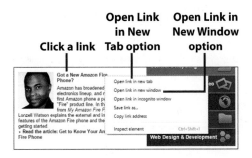

Reload a Page

If you stay on a web page too long, you may miss updates to that page's content. In addition, if a page doesn't fully or properly load, you may need to "refresh" or reload that page.

1. Click the Reload This Page button to the left of the Omnibox.

Move Forward and Back Through Pages

You can easily revisit pages you've previously displayed, and then move forward again through visited pages.

1. To move backward through previously visited pages, click the Back button.

2. To move forward through pages, click the Forward button.

Zoom In to a Page

If you're having trouble reading small text on a page, Chrome lets you increase the zoom level to make that text bigger. You can also decrease the zoom level to make the entire page smaller.

1. Click the Customize and Control button at the top right to display the drop-down menu.

2. To increase the zoom level, go to the Zoom section of the menu and click the + button.

3. To decrease the zoom level, go to the Zoom section of the menu and click the – button.

Viewing and Managing Browser History

Another way to revisit web pages you have viewed in the past is to use Google Chrome's history feature.

View Your Recent History

Chrome keeps track of your history for up to ten weeks.

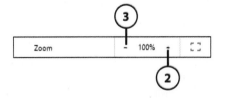

1. Click and hold the Back button.

2. This displays a list of pages you've visited in your current browsing session. To revisit a specific page, click it in the list.

View Your Full History

To revisit pages viewed on other days, you can access your full browsing history.

1. Click the Customize and Control button to display the drop-down menu; then click History.

2. The History page is now displayed in a new tab. To revisit any particular page, click that page's link.

3. To search for a particular page you've visited, enter that page's name or URL into the search box and click the Search History button.

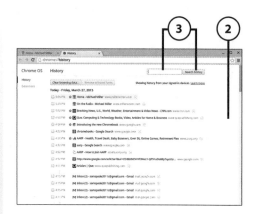

More History

To view additional pages in your history, scroll to the bottom of the page and click the Older link.

Delete Browsing History

You may not want your entire browsing history visible to others using your Chromebook—or accessing your Chrome browser on another computer. To that end, you can delete your browsing history—as well as other "tracks" to your web browsing.

Chrome lets you do any and all of the following:

- Delete browsing history (web pages you've visited).
- Delete download history (files you've downloaded).
- Empty the cache.
- Delete cookies and other site data.
- Clear saved passwords.
- Clear saved Autofill form data.

Cache

The *cache* is a local storehouse of recently visited pages. By accessing cached pages, Chrome can reload these pages faster.

Cookies

A cookie is a small text file, stored on your computer, that certain websites use to track your browsing behavior. Cookies are sometimes used to record personal data to facilitate future visits; they're also sometimes used to serve up relevant web ads.

You can clear any of these items stored in the past hour, the past day, the past week, the past four weeks, or from the beginning of time (or at least when you started using your Chromebook).

It's Not All Good

You may not want to select all the options in the Clear Browsing Data dialog box. Clearing browsing and download data erases your browsing history, so those are probably good choices. Emptying the cache is sometimes necessary, in and of itself, to clear out old versions of pages and enable you to see the most recent versions of some web pages. Deleting cookies is generally not advised, however, because this will get rid of tracking data that make some sites easier to access. And clearing saved passwords and Autofill form data might also make it less convenient to revisit pages where you've previously entered information.

1. Click the Customize and Control button to display the drop-down menu; then select More Tools, Clear Browsing Data to display the Clear Browsing Data dialog box.

2. Check those items you want to delete or clear.

3. Pull down the Obliterate the Following Items From list and select how much data to delete: past hour, past day, past week, last 4 weeks, or from the beginning of time.

4. Click the Clear Browsing Data button.

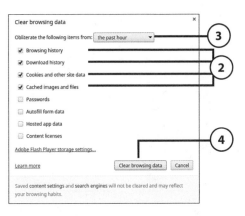

Searching the Web

As mentioned previously, Google Chrome's Omnibox functions not only as an Address box but also as a search box for searching the Web. That is, you can also use the Omnibox to enter a search query and send your search to Google or another search engine.

Enter a Query

You use the Omnibox to enter search queries that are then sent to your favorite web search engine. By default, your queries are sent to Google, so it should be a familiar experience.

1. Enter your search query into the Omnibox at the top of the browser window.

2. As you start typing in the Omnibox, Google suggests both queries and web pages you are likely to visit in a drop-down list. Select the query you want from the drop-down list.

3. Alternatively, finish typing your query and then press Enter.

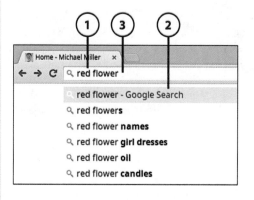

Your search results are now displayed in the browser window.

Google Search Page
You can also, of course, do your searching from Google's main search page on the Web (www.google.com). However, you get the exact same results as you do when searching from Chrome's Omnibox.

Understand Search Results

After you enter your search query, Google searches its index for all the web pages that match your query. Then it displays the results on a search results page.

Interestingly, each results page is unique; what you see depends on what you're searching for. In fact, the same query made on different days, or by different users, might return different results. That's just Google's way of trying to serve the best results for each individual user.

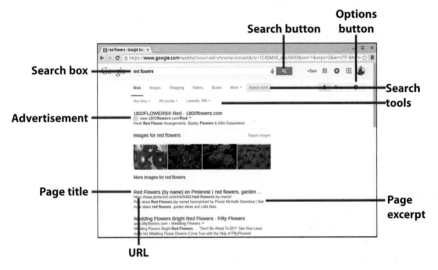

That said, there are some common elements you're likely to encounter as a result of a Google Search. These include the following:

- **Search tools**—Click the Search Tools button to display additional filtering options for your specific search. Depending on the type of search you conducted, you may have the option of filtering results by age (time), type of results (visited pages, reading levels, and so on), physical location, size or color of image, and so forth.

- **Ads**—These are paid ads by Google's advertisers. You should not confuse these ads with the "organic" search results because they may have only indirect relevance to your query. These ads typically are positioned to the right of the main search results, and sometimes above the main results.

- **Page title**—For each search result, Google displays the title of the page. The title is a clickable link; click it to view the linked-to page.

- **URL**—This is the full web address of the selected web page. It is *not* a clickable link; you have to click the page title to jump to the page.

- **Page excerpt**—Below the page title is an excerpt from the associated web page. This may be the first few sentences of text on the page, a summary of page contents, or something similar.

Local Searches

If Google thinks you're looking for something locally, Google will often display a map on the right side of the search results page. Local businesses that match your query are pinpointed on the map; these businesses are displayed in the search results under a "Places" heading. Click the Places heading or the map to display a full page of local results, via Google Maps.

Use Google's Advanced Search

If you want to perform a more targeted search, you can use Google's Advanced Search page. This page contains a number of options you can use to fine-tune your searches. All you have to do is make the appropriate selections on the page, and Google does all the fine-tuning for you.

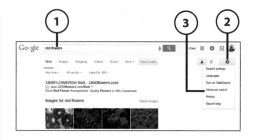

1. Perform your initial search to display the search results page.

2. Click the Options (gear) button at the top of the search results page.

3. Click Advanced Search to display the Advanced Search page.

4. Select the desired options to fine-tune your search.

5. Click the Advanced Search button at the bottom of the page to conduct your search.

What options are available on the Advanced Search page? The following table provides the details.

Options on Google's Advanced Search Page

Option	Description
Find pages with **all these words**	Google's default search mode.
Find pages with t**his exact word or phrase**	Searches for the exact phrase entered.
Find pages with **any of these words**	Searches for either one word or another, instead of for both words.
Find pages with **none of these words**	Excludes pages that contain specified word(s).
Find pages with **numbers ranging from**	Enables you to search for a range of numbers.
Narrow your results by **language**	Searches for pages written in a specific language.
Narrow your results by **region**	Narrows the search to a given country.
Narrow your results by **last update**	Enables you to search for the most recent results—past 24 hours, past week, past month, past year, or anytime.
Narrow your results by **site or domain**	Restricts the search to the specified website or domain.
Narrow your results by **terms appearing**	Restricts the search to certain areas of a page—title, text, URL, links to, or anywhere.
Narrow your results by **SafeSearch**	Filters mature content from the search results.
Narrow your results by **reading level**	Displays a graph of reading levels on the search results page; you can then click a reading level to show only those pages written at that level.
Narrow your results by **file type**	Limits the search to specific types of files.
Narrow your results by **usage rights**	Enables you to search for pages based on whether the content is free to share in various ways—not filtered by license; free to use or share; free to use or share, even commercially; free to use, share, or modify; or free to use, share, or modify, even commercially.

Additional links at the bottom of the page enable you to find pages that are similar to a given page, search pages you've previously visited, use search operators in the search box, and customize your search settings.

Change Search Providers

By default, Google Chrome uses Google for all of its browser-based searches. You can, however, change this so that you send all your queries to Yahoo! or Bing, or to another search site of your choice.

1. Click the Customize and Control button and select Settings.

2. When the Settings page appears, go to the Search section and select a provider from the pull-down list: AOL , Ask, Google, Yahoo!, or Bing.

3. To choose from additional search providers, click the Manage Search Engines button.

4. When the Search Engines panel appears, select from one of the choices in the Other Search Engines section, or enter a new search engine in the fields provided.

5. Click the Done button.

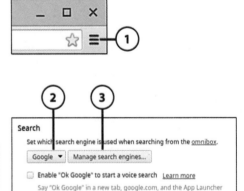

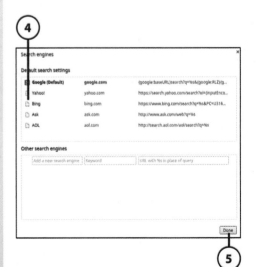

Managing Your Home Page

In a traditional web browser, the Home page is the page that opens when you first launch the browser. With the Google Chrome OS, the Home page is the one that appears when you first turn on your Chromebook—as well as when you click the Home button next to Chrome's Omnibox.

Choose a New Home Page

By default, Chrome displays its New Tab page as its Home page. You can, however, specify any web page as Chrome's Home page.

1. From within the Chrome browser, open the page you want to set as your Home page.

2. Click the Customize and Control button and then select Settings.

3. Scroll to the bottom of the Settings page and click Show Advanced Settings.

4. In the On Startup section, check Open a Specific Page or Set of Pages.

5. Click Set Pages to display the Startup Pages panel.

6. Click the Use Current Pages button.

7. Click OK.

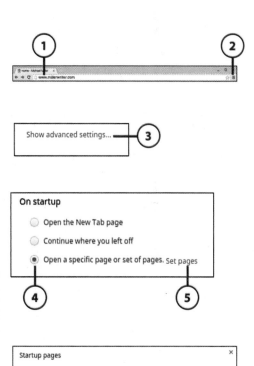

Display the Home Button

Chrome can display a Home button, next to the Omnibox, that opens the Home page when clicked. This button is not displayed by default; you'll need to enable it.

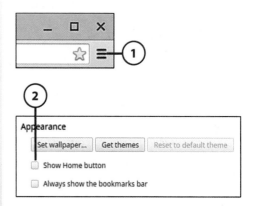

1. Click the Customize and Control button and then select Settings.

2. When the Settings page appears, go to the Appearance section and check the Show Home Button option.

Bookmarking Favorite Pages

Google Chrome lets you keep track of your favorite web pages via the use of *bookmarks*. You can bookmark the pages you want to return to in the future and display your bookmarks in a Bookmarks bar that appears just below Chrome's Omnibox.

Favorites

Google Chrome's bookmarks are the same as Internet Explorer's "Favorites."

Bookmark a Web Page

There are several ways to bookmark a web page. We'll examine the fastest method.

1. Navigate to the web page you want to bookmark.

2. Click the Bookmark This Page (star) icon in the Omnibox.

3. Chrome now bookmarks the page and displays the Bookmark Added! information bubble. Edit the name of the bookmark, if you want.

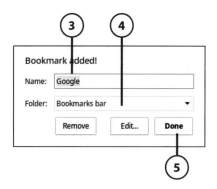

4. Pull down the Folder list to determine where you want to save this bookmark.

5. Click the Done button to save the bookmark.

Display the Bookmarks Bar

To view your bookmarks, you need to display Chrome's Bookmarks bar. This is not turned on full time; by default, it only appears at the top of the New Tab page.

You can, however, enable the Bookmarks bar so that it always appears on every open tab. It will display beneath the Omnibox.

1. Click the Customize and Control button to display the drop-down menu.

2. Select Bookmarks, Show Bookmarks Bar.

Go to a Bookmarked Page

With the Bookmarks bar visible, returning to a bookmarked page is as easy as clicking a button.

1. Click a button on the Bookmarks bar to display the bookmarked web page.

2. If you have more bookmarks than can fit in the width of the browser window, the Bookmarks bar displays a double arrow on the far-right side. Click this double arrow to display the additional bookmarks in a drop-down menu.

>>>Go Further
BOOKMARKS WITHOUT THE BAR

If you don't want to display the Bookmarks bar, there are other ways to access your bookmarks.

First, any time you display the New Tab page, the Bookmarks bar is displayed (along with thumbnails of recently visited pages). Just open a new tab and proceed from there.

You can also access your bookmarks from the Customize and Control menu. Click the Customize and Control button and then click Bookmarks; all your bookmarks are now displayed.

Manage Bookmarks

Google Chrome lets you organize your bookmarks into folders and subfolders that branch off from the Bookmarks bar, as well as in other folders on the same level as the Bookmarks bar. You do this by using Chrome's Bookmark Manager.

1. Click the Customize and Control button to display the drop-down menu and select Bookmarks, Bookmark Manager.

2. When the Bookmark Manager tab opens, the folders and subfolders of bookmarks are displayed in the left navigation pane; the individual bookmarks are displayed in the right pane. To display the contents of a folder or subfolder, select that folder in the navigation pane.

3. To change the order of bookmarks in a folder, click and drag that bookmark to a new position.

4. To move a bookmark to a different folder, drag and drop that bookmark onto the new folder.

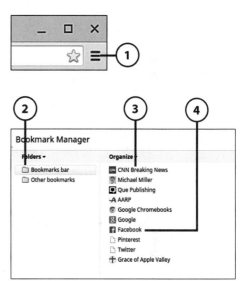

5. To list a folder's bookmarks in alphabetical order, select the folder, click the Organize button on the menu bar, and then select Reorder by Title.

6. To create a new folder or subfolder, click the Organize button and select Add Folder.

7. To edit information about a specific bookmark, select the bookmark, click the Organize button, and then select Edit. You can then edit the bookmark's name and URL from within the URL list.

8. To delete a bookmark, select that bookmark, click the Organize button, and select Delete.

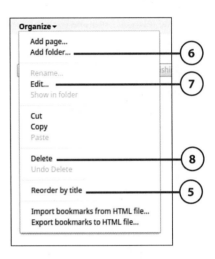

Browsing in Incognito Mode

Google Chrome, like most web browsers, keeps a record of every web page you visit. That's fine, but every now and then you might browse some web pages that you don't want tracked.

If you want or need to keep your browsing private, Google Chrome offers what it calls Incognito mode. In this special mode (actually, a separate browser window), the pages you visit aren't saved to your browser's history file, cookies aren't saved, and your activity is basically done without any record being kept.

Simultaneous Windows

Chrome lets you run both normal and Incognito windows simultaneously.

Open an Incognito Window

1. Click the Customize and Control button to display the drop-down menu; then click New Incognito Window.

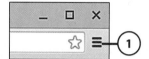

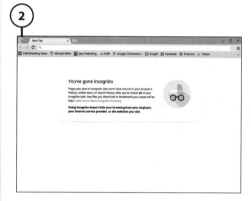

2. This opens a new Incognito window, recognizable by the little spy icon next to the first tab. You can switch between the Incognito and other open windows by pressing the Next Window button on your Chromebook's keyboard. When you are finished browsing in Incognito mode, click the X in the window's tab to close it.

Chrome Web Store

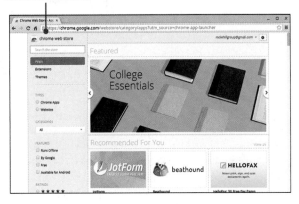

In this chapter, you learn how to add functionality to your Chromebook with Chrome apps and extensions.

→ Understanding Chrome Apps
→ Getting to Know the Chrome Web Store
→ Installing and Launching Apps
→ Managing Installed Apps
→ Installing and Using Chrome Extensions

10

Using Chrome Apps and Extensions

If you have an iPhone or Android phone, you're used to the concept of *apps*—small, single-purpose applications that you run with the touch of a button. Well, apps are also available for your Chromebook, and you can use the Chrome Web Store to find the apps you want. In addition, the Chrome Web Store offers a number of useful *extensions* that plug right in to the Chrome browser and add extra functionality to your online experience.

Understanding Chrome Apps

A Chrome app is, as the name implies, an application that you run in Google Chrome—a web-based application, to be precise. In fact, Chrome apps are actually advanced interactive websites; when you run an app, you access that website and the functionality offered there. The app runs entirely within the Chrome browser.

For example, the app called Google Calendar is a web-based calendar and scheduling application. You access the app from Google Chrome, and it looks and acts like a regular application, but the app itself is hosted on Google's website, as is all your personal calendar and appointment data.

That said, Google ensures that Chrome apps look and act like the apps on your smartphone. They are always available to you, no matter what computer you're using. Find an app you like and you can run it on your Chromebook as well as within the Chrome browser on a Windows or Mac PC.

Here's something else: Apps are always up to date. When you run an app, you're running the current version offered by that website. No time-consuming (or costly) updates or upgrades are necessary.

On your Chromebook, you easily access your apps by clicking the Launcher icon on the Shelf. This displays the Launcher panel; click All Apps to display the Apps panel, which displays all the apps installed on your Chromebook. Click the tabs at the bottom of the panel to display the next page of apps, or use the Search box to search for a specific app. Click any app to launch it in a browser window or tab.

Apps panel

Click to view apps on this tab

What kinds of Chrome apps are available? The list is long, and includes apps for listening to music, doing office work, editing photos, and even playing games. You can find a large selection of apps—most of them downloadable for free—in Google's Chrome Web Store.

Getting to Know the Chrome Web Store

The Chrome Web Store is an online marketplace, hosted by Google, where you can browse and download thousands of different apps, extensions, and themes for Google Chrome. To visit the Chrome Web Store, open the Apps panel and click the Web Store icon.

Browse the Chrome Web Store

Some of the items in the Chrome Web Store are developed by Google, others by various third-party developers. Most of these apps, extensions, and themes can run on any Chromebook; others can run on any Windows or Mac computer within the Chrome web browser.

Within the Chrome Web Store, you can browse for items by category, or search for items using the top-of-page search box. Each item in the Web Store has its own information page, where you can read more about the item, contribute your own rating and review, and download the item to your Chromebook.

Virtually all extensions and themes in the Chrome Web Store are free, as are most apps, but there are some apps that cost money to download. Other apps may be free to download, but support in-app payments; that is, you may have to pay more in the future to continue using the app, or to activate enhanced functionality.

Installing and Launching Apps

As previously noted, you can find a large number of Chrome apps in the Chrome Web Store. Just click the Web Store icon in the Apps panel.

Download and Install Apps

Chrome apps are organized in the Chrome Web Store by category— Popular, Recommended for You, Popular in the US, Collections, Business Tools, Education, Entertainment, Games, Lifestyle, News & Weather, Productivity, Social & Communication, and Utilities.

1. Click the Launcher icon on the Shelf to display the Launcher panel.

2. Click All Apps to display the Apps panel.

3. Click Web Store to open the Chrome Web Store within the Chrome browser.

4. Click Apps to view only apps.

5. Click the Categories list to display a list of categories.

6. Click the right arrow next to a category to display a list of subcategories.

7. Click the category or subcategory you want.

8. Google displays all apps within the chosen category. To learn more about a specific app, click it.

9. You now see the page for the selected app. The Overview tab is displayed by default; click the Reviews tab to see what others say about this app.

10. If you opt to use this app, click the Add to Chrome button at the top of the page.

11. If prompted to confirm the installation, click the Add button.

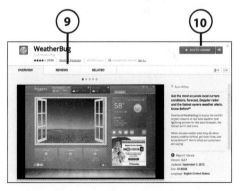

Launch Chrome Apps

After you install a Chrome app, it appears in the Apps panel. You display this panel by clicking the Launcher icon on the shelf, then clicking the All Apps icon.

1. Click the Launcher icon on the Shelf to open the Launcher panel.

2. Click the All Apps icon to open the Apps panel.

3. Click the icon for the app you want to open.

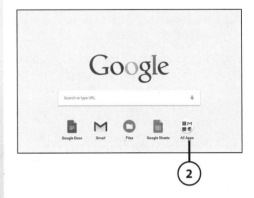

Using Chrome Apps

Like traditional desktop applications, every Chrome app is different, and works in its own unique fashion. Creating a document in Google Docs, for example, is much different from reading posts in TweetDeck or playing Angry Birds. You'll need to get to know each app you install to learn its proper usage.

Managing Installed Apps

Chrome makes it easy to manage the apps you've installed. In fact, because an app is really just a link to a web page, there's really nothing concrete to uninstall—although you can configure how apps are launched.

Determine How Apps Are Launched

By default, all Chrome apps open in a regular tab in the Chrome browser. You can change this launch behavior, however, and opt to have any given app open as follows:

- **Open as regular tab**—This is the default option.

- **Open as pinned tab**—This automatically opens a tab for the app whenever you start your Chromebook; the tab for the app is always there in the Chrome browser. (Pinned apps have smaller tabs than regular tabs, and always appear first on the row of tabs; plus, they can't be closed.)

- **Open as window**—This opens a new window for the app when you launch it.

- **Open maximized**—This launches the app in full-screen mode—actually, as a normal tab but viewed full screen.

You can select launch options for any app installed on your Chromebook.

1. Open the Apps panel.
2. Right-click the item and select from one of the Open options.

Uninstall Apps

If you find you're not using a given app, you can remove the link to that app from the Apps panel.

1. Open the Apps panel.

2. Right-click the item to delete and select Remove from Chrome.

3. When asked to confirm the removal, click the Remove button.

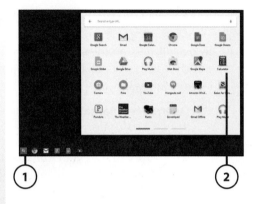

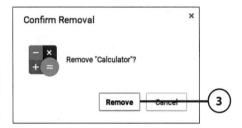

Installing and Using Chrome Extensions

Google Chrome is an interesting operating system in that Google encourages outside developers to add increased functionality. This is done via the use of *extensions* that install within Chrome and let you perform specific tasks.

For example, you can add Chrome extensions to block web page ads, display how many unread messages you have in your Gmail inbox, view status updates on Facebook or Twitter, view dictionary definitions, and capture screenshots of web pages. Thousands of these extensions are available, and they're all free.

You can find Chrome extensions in the Chrome Web Store; just scroll down and click Extensions in the left sidebar. From there you can use the top-of-page Search box to search for specific extensions by keyword, or browse available extensions.

Free Extensions
All the extensions in the Chrome Web Store can be downloaded for free.

Download and Install Extensions

Extensions are organized in the Chrome Web Store by category—Accessibility, Blogging, By Google, Developer Tools, Fun, News & Weather, Photos, Productivity, Search Tools, Shopping, Social & Communication, and Sports. You download and install extensions the same way you do Chrome apps.

1. From within the Chrome Web Store, click Extensions in the left sidebar.

2. Click the Category list to see the list of categories.

3. Click a category to view extensions of that type.

4. Click an extension to learn more.

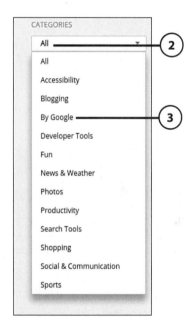

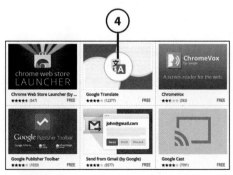

5. You now see the page for the selected extension. Read about the extension and then click the Add to Chrome button if you decide to install.

6. When asked to confirm the new extension, click the Add button.

Use Extensions

How do you use Chrome extensions? It all depends; every extension is different, although many tend to install some sort of access button next to Chrome's Omnibox. (Depending on the width of your browser window, you may need to click the more >> arrow to view the extension buttons.)

For example, the Weather extension installs a new button next to the Chrome Omnibox; this button displays the current weather and temperature. When you click the Weather button, the extension displays an information pane with your current weather conditions and forecast.

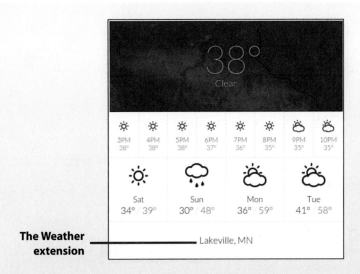

The Weather extension

You also get a new button installed when you download the Cloudy Calculator extension. Click this button and you see a scrolling calculator window, with an input field at the bottom. Enter your equation into the input field, press Enter, and the Cloudy Calculator calculates the answer for you.

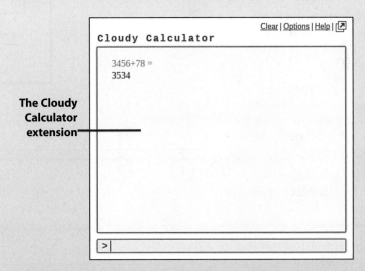

The Cloudy Calculator extension

Obviously, other extensions may work differently, but you get the picture. Add as many extensions as you like to add functionality to Chrome and your Chromebook.

Manage Chrome Extensions

Some extensions can be configured for your personal use. For example, weather-related extensions typically need your location information to display local conditions and forecasts. You can also opt to run a given extension in Chrome's Incognito anonymous browsing mode, or not.

1. Open the Chrome browser, click the Customize and Control button to display the drop-down menu, and then click More Tools > Extensions.

2. This opens the Extensions page; all the extensions you've downloaded are listed here. If you want the extension to be available when browsing in Incognito mode, check the Allow in Incognito box.

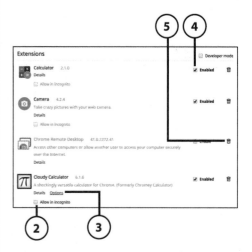

3. If an extension has configurable options, it displays an Options link; click this link to configure the options. (Not all extensions have configurable options.)

4. To disable a given extension, uncheck the Enabled box for that extension.

5. To totally delete the extension from your Chromebook, click the Remove From Chrome (trashcan) icon for that extension. When asked to confirm removal, click Remove.

Enabling Disabled Extensions

You can later enable any extension you've disabled by returning to the Extensions page and clicking Enable for that extension. You cannot undelete a deleted extension; if you want it back, you'll need to reinstall it from the Chrome Web Store.

>>>Go Further
APPS VS. EXTENSIONS: WHICH IS WHICH?

Chrome extensions seem similar to Chrome apps in that they both offer some sort of added functionality not present in Chrome itself. In reality, they are much different.

A Chrome app is a freestanding web-based application that helps you perform a specific task. Apps exist on external websites, not within the browser. You run an app when you need to run it, and not before.

A Chrome extension, on the other hand, is a plug-in for the Chrome OS or Chrome browser that adds features and functionality. Extensions are installed within Chrome, and they run automatically whenever Chrome is running.

So an app is something separate from Chrome, whereas an extension is something that runs within Chrome. In addition, apps tend to be larger in scope, whereas extensions tend to be very specific in the functionality offered.

In reality, you'll probably use both apps and extensions with your Chromebook. Extensions are great for adding little features to the OS, whereas apps are necessary for performing larger tasks, such as word processing and scheduling. You should check out some of both.

Chrome OS Image Editor

In this chapter, you learn how to view and edit digital photos on your Chromebook.

→ Viewing and Editing Photos in Chrome OS
→ Editing Photos with Adobe Photoshop Express Editor

Viewing and Editing Photos

If you take a lot of pictures with your digital camera, you're used to touching up those photos with Adobe Photoshop Elements or some similar photo-editing program. Because you can't install a photo-editing program on your Chromebook, you have to do your photo editing online.

Fortunately, you can use several cloud-based photo-editing services with your Chromebook. In addition, you can use your Chromebook to view photos stored online, or on your camera's memory card or other external storage device.

Viewing and Editing Photos in Chrome OS

Let's look first at how you can view digital photos on your Chromebook. You can view photos stored locally (in your Chromebook's long-term storage, on your camera's memory card, on a USB drive, or on an external hard drive) or online, via a cloud-based storage service or photo-sharing service.

View Photos Locally

You access photos stored on your Chromebook or on any connected storage device via the Files app.

1. Click the Launcher icon to open the Launcher panel.

2. Click All Apps to open the Apps panel.

3. Click the Files icon to launch the Files app.

4. Click the device or folder where the photos are stored. (If the photos are stored on your Chromebook, click Downloads.)

5. Click the thumbnail view button to view thumbnails of the stored pictures.

6. Click the photo you want to view.

7. Click the Open button. The photo is now displayed full screen.

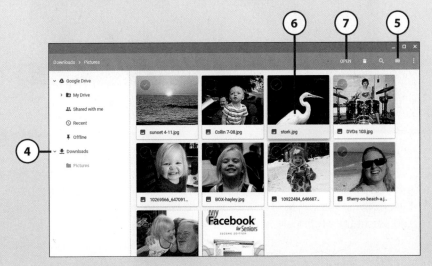

8. Mouse over the photo to see the navigation controls.

9. To view the next picture in this folder, click the right arrow or press the right-arrow button on your keyboard.

10. To view the previous picture in this folder, click the left arrow or press the left-arrow button on your keyboard.

11. To go directly to another picture in this folder, click that picture's thumbnail.

12. To view all the pictures in this folder inv a mosaic, click the Mosaic View button.

13. To view all the pictures in this folder in a slideshow, click the Slideshow button.

14. To print this photo, click the Print button.

15. To delete this photo, click the Delete button.

16. To close the photo-viewing screen, click the X at the top-right corner.

Edit Photos with the Image Editor

Chrome OS includes an Image Editor with rudimentary photo-editing functionality. You can apply an "auto fix" to any photo, as well as crop, rotate, and adjust the brightness of a photo.

1. Open the picture you want to edit; then mouse over the photo and click the Edit button to display the editing controls.

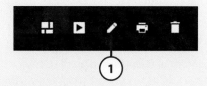

2. To overwrite your original picture file, check the Overwrite Original option. Uncheck this option to save your changes in a new file.

3. To apply the auto-fix control, click Auto-Fix.

4. To rotate the picture counterclockwise, click the Left button.

5. To rotate the picture clockwise, click the Right button.

6. To crop the photo, click the Crop button to display the crop area onscreen.

7. To fix the aspect ratio for a standard photo print, click one of the available options—1×1, 6×4, 7×5, or 16×9.

8. To move the crop area to a different part of the photo, click and drag the selection.

9. To resize the crop area manually, click and drag one of the corner selection handles.

10. To apply the crop, press Enter.

11. To adjust the brightness of the photo, click the Brightness button to display the Brightness and Contrast controls.

12. To increase the picture's brightness, drag the Brightness slider to the right. To make the picture darker, drag the Brightness slider to the left.

13. To increase the contrast of the picture, drag the Contrast slider to the right. To decrease the contrast, drag the Contrast slider to the left.

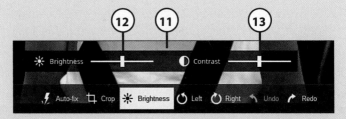

14. To apply your changes, press Enter.

View Photos Stored Online

You can also use your Chromebook to view photos stored on Google Drive, Microsoft OneDrive, and other cloud-based storage services. Photos can also be viewed on any of the popular photo storage sites, such as Flickr (www.flickr.com) and Picasa Web Albums (picasaweb.google.com).

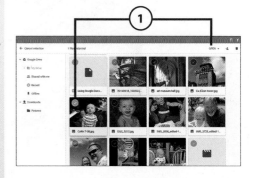

1. To view a picture stored on Google Drive, open the Files app, click My Drive in the Google Drive section of the left sidebar, navigate to and select the photo, and then click Open. You now have the same viewing and editing options as you do with photos stored on your Chromebook.

2. To view a photo stored on
another online site, use the
Chrome browser to navigate to
that site and access the photos
stored there.

Editing Photos with Adobe Photoshop Express Editor

If you want more sophisticated photo-editing options than provided by the
Chrome OS Image Editor, check out Adobe's Photoshop Express Editor
(www.photoshop.com/tools/). This web-based photo editor has a
stellar lineage, coming from the same company that brings you the full-
featured Photoshop, the number-one photo-editing program for serious
photographers. As the name implies, Photoshop Express Editor is kind of a
quick and dirty version of the full-featured Photoshop program, with all the
basic editing controls you need to fix the most common photo problems.
And, best of all, it's completely free to use.

Photoshop Express Editor offers far and away the largest collection of editing
and enhancement options of any online photo editor. Suffice it to say, just
about anything that's wrong with a photo you can fix online with Photoshop
Express Editor.

Adobe lets you store up to 2GB of photos at any time. And, like many other
web-based photo editors, Photoshop Express Editor is integrated with Flickr,
so you can upload your edited photos to the Flickr site with a minimum of
fuss and muss.

>>>Go Further
OTHER ONLINE PHOTO EDITORS

Although Photoshop Express Editor is an impressive (and free) service, several other free online photo editors are worth checking out. These include the following:

- FotoFlexer (www.fotoflexer.com)
- PicMonkey (www.picmonkey.com)
- Picture2Life (www.picture2life.com)
- Pixlr Express and Pixlr Editor (www.pixlr.com)
- Sumo Paint (www.sumopaint.com)

Pixlr is a particularly powerful photo-editing site, rivaling Adobe's full-featured Photoshop in functionality. You have the ability to edit layers and do other sophisticated photo-editing tasks, which more advanced photographers will appreciate.

Edit a Photo

Photoshop Express Editor is a cloud-based app that you access from the Chrome web browser.

1. From the Chrome web browser, go to www.photoshop.com/tools/.

2. Click Start the Editor to display the Select a Photo to Edit pane.

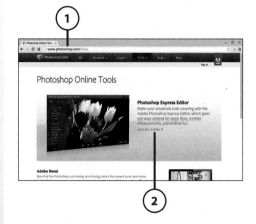

3. Click Upload Photo.

4. When the next dialog box appears, click the Upload button to open the Chrome Files app.

5. Navigate to and select the photo you want to edit, either on your Chromebook or on Google Drive.

6. Click Open to display the picture in Photoshop Express Editor.

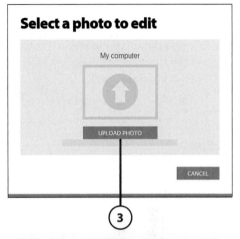

3

4

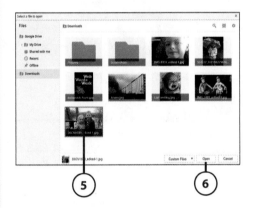

5   6

Crop a Picture

Once a picture is loaded in the editor, you can begin editing the picture. One of the most common options is to crop the picture so that only a smaller part of the image is visible.

1. From Photoshop Express Editor, make sure that Edit is selected in the left panel; then go to the Basic section and click Crop & Rotate. The picture appears with crop handles at each corner.
2. Click the Crop Dimensions button and select the desired aspect ratio (such as 4 × 6 or 8 × 10). For a custom size, select Freeform.
3. Click and drag the crop handles until you like what you see onscreen.
4. Click Done.

Rotate a Picture

Sometimes a photograph appears sideways and needs to be rotated. You can easily do this with Photoshop Express Editor.

1. Make sure that Edit is selected; then, in the left panel, go to the Basic section and click Crop & Rotate.
2. In the Rotate & Flip section, click the Rotate Left button to rotate the picture counterclockwise 90 degrees.
3. Click the Rotate Right button to rotate the picture clockwise 90 degrees.
4. Click Done.

Remove Red Eye

The red eye effect sometimes results when a camera's flash is too close to the eyes of the subject. You can remove red eye using Photoshop Express Editor.

1. Make sure that Edit is selected; then, in the Basic section of the left panel, click Red-Eye.

2. Click the eye you want to change. Repeat for all red eyes in the photo.

3. Click Done.

Zoom

You can better see small details (such as red eyes) by zooming in to a photo. Click the Zoom button at the bottom of the screen to display the Zoom slider; click and drag the slider up to zoom in to the picture, or down to zoom out.

Apply Auto Correct

Some pictures can benefit from a slight fine tuning of color, brightness, and contrast. To apply an automatic fix for these elements, use Photoshop Express Editor's Auto Correct control.

1. Make sure that Edit is selected; then, in the Basic section of the left panel, click Auto Correct.

2. You now see a selection of thumbnails at the top of the editing window. Click the thumbnail that looks best to you.

3. Click Done.

Adjust Exposure

When a picture is underexposed, it appears too dark. When a picture is overexposed, it appears too light. You can adjust the exposure of any picture from within Photoshop Express Editor.

1. Make sure that Edit is selected; then, in the Basic section of the left panel, click Exposure.

2. You now see a selection of thumbnails at the top of the editing window, from dark to light. The darker thumbnails apply a lower exposure, whereas the lighter ones apply a higher exposure. Click the thumbnail that looks best to you.

3. Click Done.

Adjust Color Saturation

Photoshop Express Editor can adjust the color saturation of a photo, anywhere from no color (black and white) to too much color.

1. Make sure that Edit is selected; then, in the Basic section of the left panel, click Saturation.

2. You now see a selection of thumbnails at the top of the editing window, from undersaturated to oversaturated. Click the thumbnail that looks best to you.

3. Click Done.

Apply Advanced Adjustments

Adobe Photoshop Express Editor also includes a variety of more advanced adjustments useful to professional photographers. You can adjust white balance, highlight, fill light, dodge, burn, sharpen, and soft focus settings.

1. From within Photoshop Express Editor, with Edit selected, go to the Adjustments section in the left panel and click the adjustment you want to apply.

2. Some adjustments present you with a series of thumbnails representing different levels of that adjustment. Click the thumbnail you want.

3. Other adjustments have their own controls. Use the controls to apply the effect.

4. Click Done.

Apply Special Effects

Photoshop Express Editor offers a variety of special effects you can apply to any photograph. These effects include crystalize, pixelate, pop color, hue, black & white, tint, sketch, and distort.

1. From within Photoshop Express Editor, with Edit selected, go to the Effects section in the left panel and click the effect you want to apply.

2. Some effects present you with a series of thumbnails representing different applications of that effect. Click the thumbnail you want.

3. Other effects present additional choices. Use the controls to select the desired effect.

4. Click Done.

>>>Go Further
PHOTOSHOP CC ONLINE

Although Adobe's Photoshop Express Editor is fine for most casual shutterbugs, more advanced photographers need all the powerful tools built in to the full-featured version of Photoshop. Up till now, you could only get this functionality from Adobe's Photoshop Creative Cloud (CC) software—but that's about to change.

Adobe is currently testing an online version of the full-featured Photoshop CC. Although it's not yet available to the general public, look for this high-powered photo-editing app to be launched in the near future. It will be of particular interest to Chromebook owners because it requires no hardware installation to run.

Interestingly, this online version of Photoshop is not a cloud-based app, where the software resides in the cloud but runs in your local browser. Instead, this new version of Photoshop is a network streaming application. The software itself runs on Google's central Compute Engine servers and then streams the screen contents over the Internet to your Chromebook, using a modified version of Google's Remote Desktop extension. Your Chromebook then sends mouse clicks and keystrokes, in real time, back to the server for interpretation.

It's a very interesting approach to cloud computing, much different from anything else in use today. If it works (and it's still in testing, remember), expect other powerful programs to adopt this approach, delivering even more functionality to the universe of Chromebook users.

Know, however, that unlike Photoshop Express Editor, which is available for free to anyone, the new online version of Photoshop CC is likely to be available only to users who subscribe to Adobe's Photoshop Creative Cloud service. That means you'll have to pay for it—but you'll be getting a lot of functionality for your money.

Watching a movie with Netflix

In this chapter, you learn how to view movies, TV shows, and other videos on your Chromebook.

→ Watching Streaming Video on Your Chromebook
→ Purchasing and Renting Videos from Google Play
→ Viewing Locally Stored Videos
→ Watching Videos on YouTube

12

Viewing Movies, TV Shows, and Other Streaming Video

Many television viewers are "cutting the cord" by disconnecting from cable service and instead watching their favorite programs online, on their computers. Not surprisingly, it's easy to use your Chromebook to watch television shows and movies online, via Netflix, Hulu, and other streaming video services.

Watching Streaming Video on Your Chromebook

There's a ton of programming on the Web that you don't have to purchase or download as large video files. This programming is available via a technology called *streaming video*, which is perfect for viewing on your Chromebook. It works by streaming the movie or TV show you pick over the Internet in real time to your Chromebook; you, then, watch the programming in the Chrome browser. You can find tens of thousands of free and paid videos to watch at dozens of different websites.

View Movies and TV Shows on Netflix

When it comes to watching movies and TV shows online, you can't beat Netflix, a streaming video service with more than 57 million subscribers. Netflix lets you watch all the movies and TV shows you want, all for a low $7.99/month subscription.

Netflix offers a mix of classic and newer movies. In addition, you'll find a wide range of TV programming, from *The Dick Van Dyke Show* to *Marvel's Agents of Shield*.

You watch Netflix in the Chrome browser, from the Netflix website.

DVD Rental
Netflix also offers a separate DVD-by-mail rental service, with a separate subscription fee.

1. Open the Chrome browser and go to www.netflix.com.

2. If you have an existing account, click the Sign In button and then enter your username and password.

3. If you do not have an existing account, you need to create one. Click Start Your Free Month and follow the onscreen instructions to create your account and receive your first month free.

4. If you have multiple users on your Netflix account, you'll be prompted to select a user. Do so.

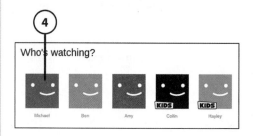

5. You now see Netflix's main screen. Scroll down to see suggestions based on what's popular and what you've recently watched.

6. To search for a specific program, click Search, enter the name of the program, and then press Enter.

7. To browse by category, click Browse to display a list of categories.

8. Click the category you want to view.

9. Click the thumbnail for the TV show or movie you want.

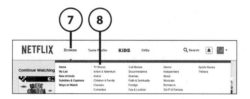

10. The video now begins playing. (If you chose a TV show, the first—or next—episode plays.) Mouse over the screen to display the playback controls.

11. Click Pause to pause playback; the Pause button changes to a Play button. Click Play to resume playback.

12. Click and drag the slider (scrubber) control to move to another segment of the program.

13. Click the Fullscreen button to display the program full screen. Press Esc to return to normal viewing in your browser.

14. To choose a different episode of a TV series, tap the Series button to display available seasons and episodes and then make your selection.

Watching TV Shows

If you choose to watch a TV show, you typically can choose from different episodes in different seasons. Select a season to see all episodes from that season and then click the episode you want to watch.

>>>Go Further

NETWORK TV PROGRAMMING

Most major broadcast and cable TV networks offer their shows for viewing from their websites. These include ABC (abc.go.com), CBS (www.cbs.com), Comedy Central (www.comedycentral.com), CW (www.cwtv.com), Fox (www. fox.com), NBC (www.nbc.com), Nick (www.nick.com), TNT (www.tntdrama. com), and USA Network (www.usanetwork.com).

View TV Shows on Hulu

If Netflix is the best website for movies and classic TV shows, Hulu is the best site for newer television programming. Hulu offers episodes from a number of major-network TV shows, as well as some new and classic feature films. (There is also a fair number of programs from Canada, England, and other countries.) The standard free membership offers access to a limited number of videos; Hulu Plus ($7.99/month) offers a larger selection of newer shows.

As with Netflix, you watch Hulu in the Chrome browser, from the Hulu website.

1. Open the Chrome browser and go to www.hulu.com.

2. Click Log In.

3. If you have an existing account, enter your email address and password; then click Log In. (You can also log in with your Facebook account.)

4. If you do not have an existing account, you need to create one. Click Sign Up for Free and follow the onscreen instructions from there.

5. Hulu's home page displays a variety of featured programs. Scroll down to view recommended programming by type.

6. To view television programs, click TV at the top of the page.

7. To view programs by genre, click the Genres tile.

8. To search for a specific show, enter the name of the show into the top-of-page Search box and then press Enter.

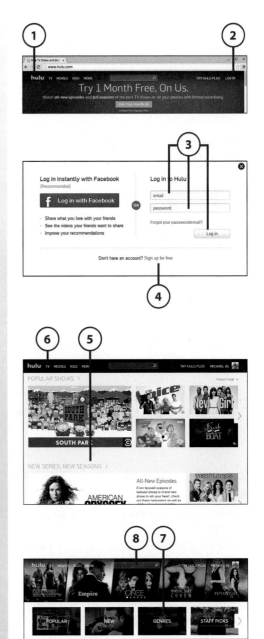

9. Click the tile for the show you want to watch.

10. When the detailed program page appears, scroll down to view available episodes, clips, and extras.

11. Click the tile for the episode you want to watch.

12. Hulu begins playing the program you selected. Move your mouse over the screen to display the playback controls.

13. Click the Pause button to pause playback; the Pause button changes to a Play button. Click the Play button to resume playback.

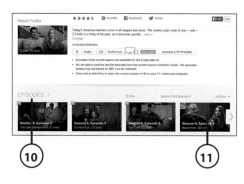

14. Click and drag the slider (scrubber) control to move to another segment of the program.

15. Click the Fullscreen button to view the program full screen on your Chromebook. Press Esc to exit full-screen mode.

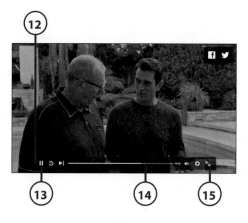

Movies

Hulu also offers a variety of movies for online viewing. The standard free membership has a very limited selection of movie programming, typically documentaries and movie trailers. The $7.99 Hulu Plus membership offers a much larger selection of movies.

>>>*Go Further*
WATCHING NETFLIX AND HULU ON YOUR LIVING ROOM TV

Watching movies and TV shows on your Chromebook is fine when you're on the go, but it's not the same as watching programming on the flat screen TV you have in your living room. To that end, you can connect most Chromebooks to your living room TV, with a single cable.

If your Chromebook has an HDMI output (and most do), it's easy to connect an HDMI cable between your Chromebook and your living room TV. (HDMI is the cable technology used to connect high-definition Blu-ray players, cable boxes, and other equipment to flat screen TVs; the HDMI cable carries both audio and video signals.) Once you have the cable connected, start Netflix or Hulu on your Chromebook, as you would normally, and then switch your TV to the corresponding HDMI input. The programming you're playing on your Chromebook is now displayed on your TV. Sit back and start watching.

Purchasing and Renting Videos from Google Play

Netflix, Hulu, and the like are great, but they don't always offer the most recent hit movies. (You wouldn't expect them to, at their low monthly subscription prices.) If you want to see a flick fresh from the movie theater, you need to purchase it or rent it—which you can do online, from the Google Play Movies store.

Purchase or Rent a Video

You access Google Play from the Play Movies app on your Chromebook. You can then purchase new videos or watch videos you've previously purchased.

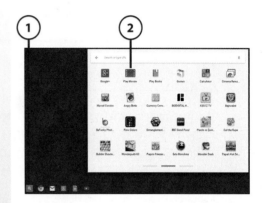

1. Open the Apps panel.

2. Click Play Movies to open the Google Play Movies app.

3. Click Shop.

4. This opens the Google Play store in the Chrome browser. To browse available movies, click Movies in the left sidebar.

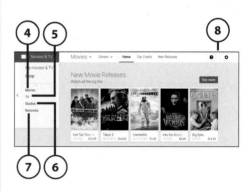

5. To view available TV shows, click TV in the left sidebar.

6. To browse by movie studio or production studio, click Studios in the left sidebar.

7. To browse by television or cable network, click Networks in the left sidebar.

8. To search for a specific movie or show, enter the name of the program into the search box at the top of the screen and then press Enter.

9. You now see the detail page for the movie or show you selected. To purchase the movie for download to your Chromebook, click the Buy button.

10. Many items let you rent the program for a lower price. Most rentals need to be viewed within 30 days; once you start watching, you typically have 48 hours to finish. Click the Rent button to rent the item.

11. Click the appropriate Buy or Rent button to complete the transaction. If you have the choice of buying/renting in high definition (HD) or standard definition (SD), click the appropriate button. The item is now added to your Google Play library.

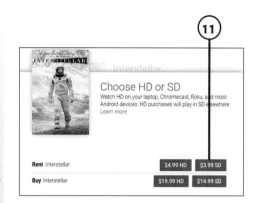

SD vs. HD

For viewing on your Chromebook, select SD. That's because most Chromebooks cannot play back in HD quality, so you shouldn't pay extra for something you can't get. Some higher-end Chromebooks have higher resolution displays, for which HD is a more appropriate (but also more costly) choice.

Watch a Google Play Video

You watch movies or shows you've purchased or rented from the Google Play Movies app. Google stores your items online and then streams them to your Chromebook when you're ready to watch them.

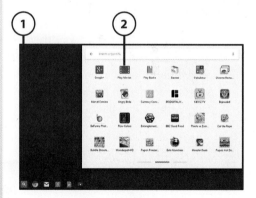

1. Open the Apps panel.

2. Click Play Movies to open the Google Play Movies app.

3. To see movies you've purchased or rented, click My Movies.

4. To see television programming you've purchased or rented, click My TV Shows.

5. Click the item you want to watch.

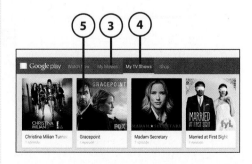

6. Playback begins in the Play Movies window. Mouse over the screen to display the playback controls.

7. Click the Pause button to pause playback; the Pause button changes to a Play button. Click the Play button to resume playback.

8. Click and drag the slider (scrubber) control to move to another segment of the program.

9. Click the Fullscreen button to view the program full screen on your Chromebook. Press Esc to exit full-screen mode.

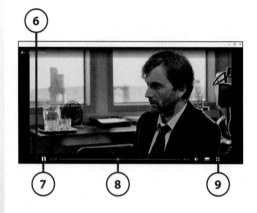

Viewing Locally Stored Videos

If you have home movies or other videos on some sort of external storage device, you can easily view them on your Chromebook—as long as the individual video is in an approved file format. At present, Chrome supports videos encoded in the .mp4, .mpv, .mov, and .webm file formats, as well as Ogg Vorbis video files.

1. Insert the external storage device into your Chromebook.

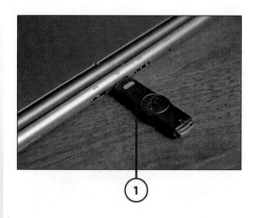

2. When the Files app opens, open the folder for the external storage device and navigate to the subfolder where the video file is stored.

3. Click the video file you want to view.

4. Click the Open button.

5. The video begins playback in the Media Player window. Mouse over the video to display the playback controls.

6. To pause playback, click the Pause button; the Pause button changes to a Play button. Click the Play button to resume playback.

7. To view the video full screen on your desktop, click the Fullscreen button.

8. To advance to another section of the video, drag the scrubber to the right (forward) or the left (backward).

9. To close the Media Player window, click the X at the top-right corner.

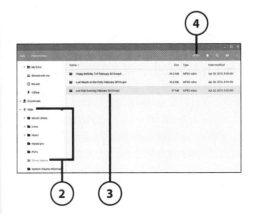

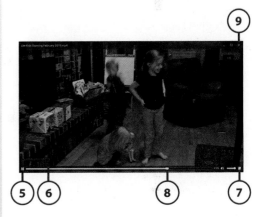

Watching Videos on YouTube

Google also makes it easy to watch videos from its YouTube subsidiary. YouTube (www.youtube.com) contains millions of videos uploaded by both companies and individuals; it's a great place to find just about anything in video format, and it's totally free.

1. Click the YouTube button on the desktop Shelf, or in the Apps panel.

2. The YouTube home page displays in the Chrome browser. You should automatically be signed in to YouTube with your Google Account. (If not, click the Sign In button and sign in.)

3. Browse or search for a video you wish to watch.

4. Click the video's thumbnail to begin playback on a new page.

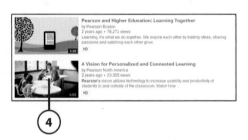

5. Click Pause to pause playback; the Pause button changes to a Play button. Click Play to resume playback.

6. Click anywhere on the red scrubber to move to a different place in the video.

7. To view the video full screen, click the Full Screen button.

Vimeo

Vimeo (www.vimeo.com) is another popular video-sharing website. There's a nice Vimeo app in the Chrome Web Store that many Chromebook users seem to like.

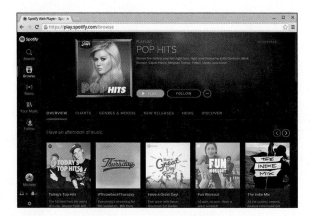

Listening to music with Spotify

13

Listening to Music

Many people like to listen to music on their Chromebooks. Maybe it's a little background music while you're browsing Facebook or working on a Google Docs document. Or maybe your Chromebook is your primary source of music, blasting your favorite tunes across the entire room. In any case, you can use your Chromebook to listen to tunes you've downloaded or those streamed across the Internet from Spotify, Pandora, and similar services.

Listening to Streaming Music Services

It used to be that music lovers bought vinyl albums and singles. Sometime in the mid-1980s, they switched to buying digital compact discs. Then, at the turn of the century, there was another shift, to downloading digital music over the Internet.

Today, another shift is in progress. Instead of buying music one track or album at a time, more and more people are subscribing to online music services that let you listen to all the songs you want, either for free or a low monthly charge. These services, such as Pandora and Spotify, stream music in real time over the Internet to your Chromebook; there's nothing to download, nothing to store on your computer, and it's all perfectly legal.

>>>Go Further
ON-DEMAND VS. PERSONALIZED SERVICES

There are two primary types of delivery services for streaming audio over the Internet. The first model, typified by Pandora, is like traditional radio in that you can't dial up specific tunes; you have to listen to whatever the service beams out, but in the form of personalized playlists or virtual radio stations. The second model, typified by Spotify, lets you specify which songs you want to listen to; we call these *on-demand services*.

Listen to Pandora

Pandora is much like traditional AM or FM radio, in that you listen to the songs Pandora selects for you, along with accompanying commercials. It's a little more personalized than traditional radio however, in that you create your own personalized stations (up to 100). All you have to do is choose a song or artist; Pandora then creates a station with other songs like the one you picked. You access Pandora from the Chrome browser, at www.pandora.com.

Free vs. Paid
Pandora's basic membership is free, but ad-supported. (You have to suffer through commercials.) To get rid of the commercials, pay for the $4.99/month Pandora One subscription.

1. Open the Chrome browser and navigate to www.pandora.com.

2. If you don't yet have a Pandora account (the basic account is free), click Register and follow the onscreen instructions.

3. If you already have an account, click Sign In; then enter your email address and password.

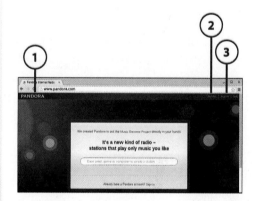

4. To create a new station, enter the name of a song, genre, artist, or composer into the Create Station box at the top-left corner and then press Enter.

5. The new station is added to your station list on the left side of the page. Click a station to begin playback; information about this track and artist is now displayed.

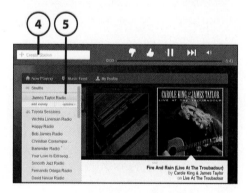

6. To pause playback, click the Pause button at the top of the page. Click Play to resume playback.

7. To like the current song, click the thumbs up button. Pandora will now play more songs like this one.

8. If you don't like the current song, click the thumbs down button. Pandora will now skip to the next song, not play the current song again, and play fewer songs like it.

9. To skip to the next song without disliking it, click the next track button.

>>>Go Further

LOCAL RADIO STATIONS ONLINE

If you'd rather just listen to your local AM or FM radio station—or to a radio station located in another city—you can do so over the Internet. Both iHeartRadio (www.iheart.com) and TuneIn (www.tunein.com) offer free access to local radio stations around the world, from within the Chrome browser.

Listen to Spotify

The other big streaming music service is Spotify. Unlike Pandora, Spotify lets you choose specific tracks to listen to.

You listen to Spotify via its web player. (It also offers a traditional software-based player, but you can't use that on a Chromebook.) The easiest way to open Spotify's web player is via the Spotify app, available from Google's Web Store.

Free vs. Paid

Spotify's basic membership is free, but you're subjected to commercials every few songs. If you want to get rid of the commercials (and get on-demand music on your mobile devices, too), you need to pay for a $9.99/month subscription.

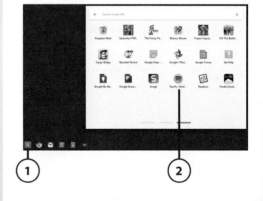

1. After installing the Spotify app from Google's Web Store, click the Launcher button on the shelf and open the Apps panel.

2. Click the Spotify icon to open the Spotify web player in the Chrome browser.

3. Click Browse in the left sidebar.

4. To browse by musical genre, click Genres & Moods to browse by musical genre.

5. Click a genre tile to view music of that type.

6. To search for a specific song, album, or artist, click Search in the left sidebar and then enter your query.

7. Click a playlist, album, or artist to view all included songs.

8. Click the green Play button to play all the songs in the playlist or album, or by that artist.

9. Double-click a song title to play that particular track.

10. Playback controls now display in a new pane on the right. Use these controls to pause, rewind, or fast-forward playback, or to raise or lower the volume.

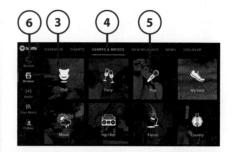

>>>Go Further
OTHER STREAMING MUSIC SERVICES

Pandora and Spotify aren't the only streaming music services on the Internet. Numerous web-based services are available that stream music to any connected device over the Internet. Many offer Chrome apps for their services; those that don't have apps can be accessed from the Chrome web browser.

The list of popular streaming music services includes the following:

- Beats Music (www.beatsmusic.com)
- Google Play Music All Access (play.google.com/about/music/)
- Rdio (www.rdio.com)
- Rhapsody (www.rhapsody.com)
- Slacker (www.slacker.com)

Listening to Music Stored Locally or Online

If you have a lot of music downloaded in MP3 format, you can listen to that music on your Chromebook. Due to the Chromebook's limited built-in storage, you probably want to copy your tunes to a USB memory stick and then insert that storage device into your Chromebook. Chrome's built-in Audio Player app will then play the music on your storage device.

You can also listen to music you have stored online, in Google Drive. Just use Chrome's Files app to navigate to your stored files and then start listening.

It's Not All Good

Incompatibility Issues

Note that Chrome's Audio Player does not support all types of music files. It's compatible with the popular MP3 audio format, but not with Apple's .aac or Microsoft's .wma formats. So if you have your files in an iTunes library, for example, you'll first need to convert them to MP3 format to listen to them on your Chromebook.

Listen to a Single Track

We'll assume that you've already copied your favorite MP3 files to a USB memory device. You'll use that device to listen to your music on your Chromebook.

1. Open the Apps panel.

2. Click the Files icon to launch the Files app.

3. Navigate to where your music files are stored—on an external storage device or on Google Drive—and to any specific subfolder on that device.

4. Click to select the music file to which you want to listen.

5. Click the Open button.

6. This opens the Audio Player and starts playback. To pause playback, click the Pause button; to resume playback, click the Play button.

7. To close the Audio Player, click the X at the upper right corner.

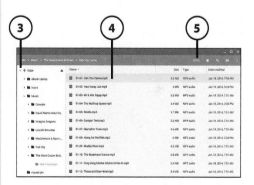

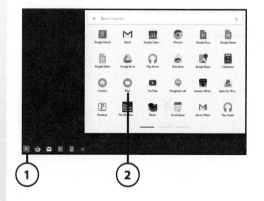

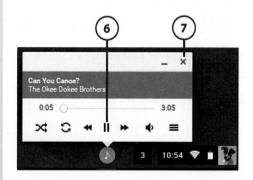

Listen to a Playlist

Chrome's Audio Player can also play back a playlist of multiple tracks. This lets you program music for an extended sitting.

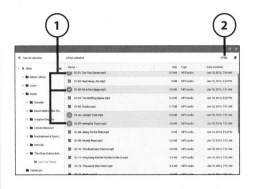

1. Open the Files app and select those music files you wish to include in the playlist. To select multiple files, hold down the Ctrl key while clicking each one.

2. Click the Open button.

3. This opens the Audio Player and starts playback of the first song in the playlist. To pause playback, click the Pause button; to resume playback, click the Play button.

4. To advance to the next song in the playlist, click the Next Track button.

5. To listen to the previous song, click the Previous Track button.

6. To view the entire playlist, click the Playlist button. This expands the Audio Player pane to display all tracks in the playlist.

Listening to Your Own Music with Google Play

Listening to your own music via an external storage device might not be ideal for all users. Many music lovers prefer to listen to streaming music over the Internet; this provides for a larger selection of music with no local storage limitations.

To this end, Google offers the Google Play Music service, which enables you to stream your own music back to you over the Internet. You can upload the favorite tracks from your personal music collection and then play them back from any web browser—including the Chrome browser on your Chromebook. You can upload and listen to up to 20,000 individual tracks, all for free.

Scan and Match
Google Play Music is actually a "scan and match" service. That is, it scans the files you want to upload, and then matches them against tracks in its own large music library. If the tracks are already there, it doesn't have to upload your tracks, thus saving you lots of time. If, on the other hand, your tracks are not in Google's library, it uploads them for your future listening pleasure.

Upload Your Music to Google Play

You can upload music files from your Chromebook or from any Windows or Mac PC, using the Google Play app.

File Formats
Google's Music Manager lets you upload audio files in the following audio formats: .mp3, .m4a/AAC, .wma (Windows only), .flac, and .ogg.

1. Open the Apps panel.

2. Click the Play Music icon to open the Google Play Music app in the Chrome browser.

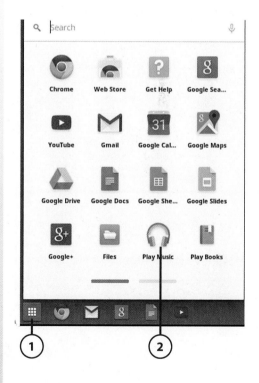

3. Click the Menu button at the top left to open the navigation sidebar.

4. Scroll down and click Add Music to open the Add Music window.

5. Click the Select From Your Computer button to display the Files app.

6. Navigate to and select the device or folder where you store your digital music.

7. Click to select the files you want to upload.

8. Click the Open button. The selected files are automatically added to your music collection.

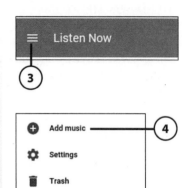

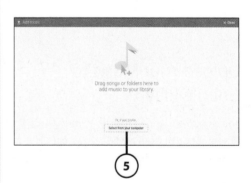

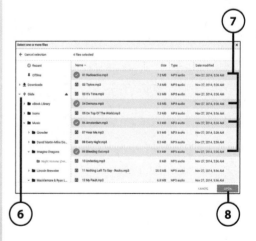

Play Music with Google Play

Once you've uploaded your music to Google Play Music, you can use your Chromebook's Chrome browser to play back your favorite tracks.

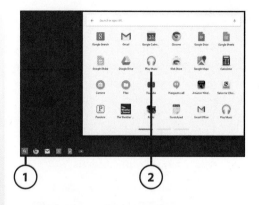

1. Open the Apps panel.

2. Click the Play Music icon to open the Google Play Music app in the Chrome browser.

3. Click the Menu button to open the navigation sidebar.

4. Click My Library.

5. At the top of the window, click to select what you want to listen to—Artists, Albums, Songs, or Genres.

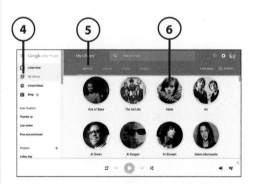

6. Select the artist, album, song, or genre you want to listen to.

7. To listen to specific songs, click to select the ones you want to listen to. (Hold down the Ctrl key to select multiple songs.)

8. Click the Play button to begin playback.

9. Click the Shuffle button to play your selections in a random order.

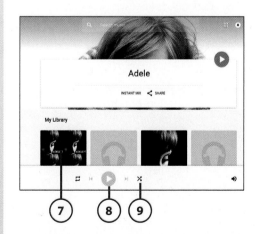

Create and Play Playlists

Google Play Music enables you to create your own custom playlists of songs, and then play back those playlists in random order.

1. From within Google Play Music, open the navigation sidebar and scroll to the Playlists section.

2. To select an existing playlist, click the name of that playlist.

3. To begin playback, click the Play button.

4. To play the playlist in random order, click the Shuffle Playlist button.

5. To create a new playlist, click the + button in the Playlists section of the sidebar.

6. When the New Playlist pane appears, enter a name for this playlist into the Name box.

7. If you want, enter a description of this playlist into the Description box.

8. Click Create Playlist.

9. To add a song to this playlist, click My Library and navigate to the album or genre where the song is located.

10. Click the More button to display the pop-up menu.

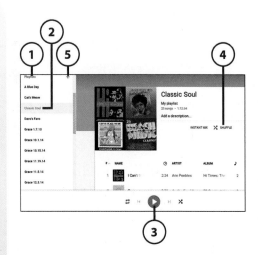

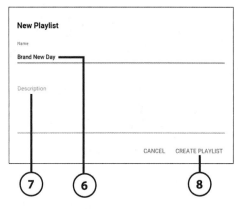

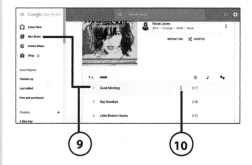

11. Click Add to Playlist to display a list of all your playlists.

12. Click the name of the playlist to which you want to add this song.

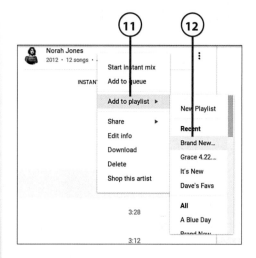

Drag and Drop
Alternatively, you can use your Chromebook's touchpad to click and drag any individual track and then drop it onto the playlist of choice in the sidebar.

Gmail inbox

In this chapter, you learn how to send and receive email with Google's Gmail service.

→ Getting to Know Gmail
→ Reading and Replying to Messages
→ Sending New Messages
→ Managing Your Messages

14

Emailing with Gmail

If you've used email on a traditional Windows or Mac computer, chances are you've used a traditional POP or IMAP email service provided by your Internet Service Provider (or your company's ISP), along with a corresponding email application, such as Microsoft Outlook. The world is moving away from POP/IMAP email, however, towards web-based email services—which are perfect for use on your Chromebook.

Unlike POP/IMAP email, web mail can be accessed from any computer or connected device, using any web browser. Even better, all your messages are stored on the Web, not locally. This lets you retrieve and manage your email when you're out of the office or on the road.

The three largest web mail services today are hosted by Google (Gmail), Microsoft (Outlook.com), and Yahoo! (Yahoo! Mail). Because you're using a Google Chromebook, Gmail is probably your email service of choice, so let's see how it works.

Getting to Know Gmail

Google's Gmail is the largest and most popular email service today. It's web-based email, which means you can access your inbox from any computer (including your Chromebook), anywhere you might happen to be.

You don't need to sign up for Gmail, because you're already signed up, by virtue of having a Google Account. Like other Google services, Gmail is completely free.

Access Gmail

You access Gmail from the Chrome browser (or from any browser on any computer, smartphone, or tablet) at mail.google.com or gmail.com. You can also access Gmail with the Gmail app included with your Chromebook. Obviously, the Gmail app is the most convenient way to do it, so click the Gmail icon on the desktop Shelf to get started. (Alternatively, you can open the Apps panel and click the Gmail icon there.)

Click to launch Gmail

Navigate Gmail

When Gmail launches, by default you see the Inbox, which contains all your received messages. You can switch to other views by clicking the appropriate links on the left side of the page. For example, to view all your sent mail, simply click the Sent Mail link on the left.

Unread message   **Tabs**

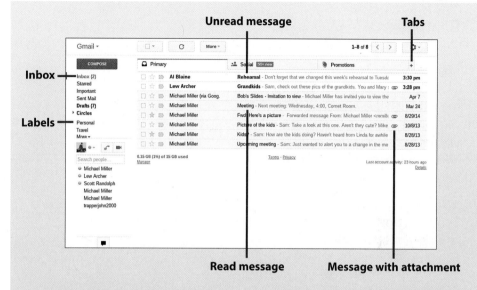

Inbox   **Labels**

Read message   **Message with attachment**

Gmail attempts, though not always successfully, to organize your incoming mail by type and display each type of message on a separate tab. The Primary tab displays standard correspondence; the Social tab displays messages from Facebook, Google+, and other social networks; and the Promotions tab displays advertising email. You can also display tabs for Updates (messages from companies and services you use on a regular basis) and Forums (messages from web forums); click the + tab and select which tabs you want to display. Click a tab to read all messages of a given type.

Reading and Replying to Messages

You receive and read all your incoming messages in the Gmail inbox. Each message is listed with the message's sender, the message's subject, a snippet from the message, and the date or time the message was sent. (The snippet typically is the first line of the message text.)

Read Messages

Unread inbox messages are listed in bold; after a message has been read, it's displayed in normal, nonbold text with a shaded background. And if you've assigned a label to a message (discussed later in this chapter), the label appears before the message subject.

Group Actions

To perform an action on a message or group of messages in the inbox, such as deleting them, put a check mark by the message(s), and then click one of the buttons at the top of the list. Alternatively, you can click the More button to display a list of additional actions to perform.

1. Click the tab for the type of message you want to view. (Most of your important messages will be on the Primary tab.)

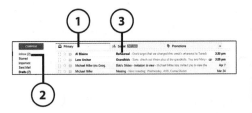

2. Click the Inbox link on the left to display all incoming messages.

3. Click the header for the message you want to view. This displays the full text of the message on a new page.

4. To print the message, click the Print All icon.

5. To return to the Inbox, click the Back to Inbox button.

View Conversations

One of the unique things about Gmail is that all related email messages are grouped in what Google calls *conversations*. A conversation might be an initial message and all its replies (and replies to replies). A conversation might also be all the daily emails from a single source with a common subject, such as messages you receive from subscribed-to mailing lists.

A conversation is noted in the Inbox list by a number in parentheses after the sender name(s). If a conversation has replies from more than one person, more than one name is listed.

1. To view a conversation, simply click the message title. The most recent message displays in full.

2. To view the text of any individual message in a conversation, click that message's header.

3. To expand *all* the messages in a conversation, click the Expand All link. All the messages in the conversation are stacked on top of each other, with the text of the newest message fully displayed.

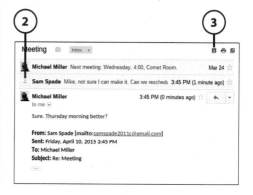

View Pictures and Other Attachments

Many people use email to send pictures and other files to their friends, family, and colleagues. These files are attached to an email message and are called *attachments*. If a message has a file attached, you'll see a paperclip icon next to the message in the inbox.

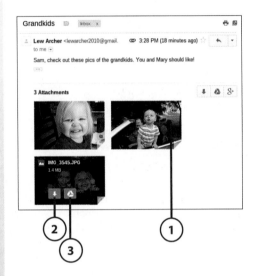

1. When viewing a message, you see any attached photos as thumbnail images. Click a thumbnail to view the picture full size in Chrome's photo viewer.

2. To download an attached folder or file, mouse over the item and then click the Download icon.

3. To save an attached file to Google Drive, mouse over the item and then click the Save to Drive icon.

Reply to Messages

Whether you're reading a single message or a conversation, it's easy to reply to that message.

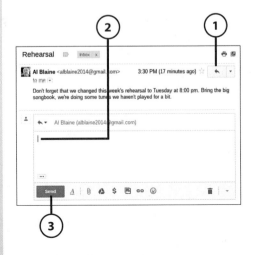

1. In the original message, click the Reply button to expand the message to include a reply box.

2. Add your new text into the reply box.

3. To send the message, click the Send button.

Reply to All

If a conversation has multiple participants, you can reply to all of them by clicking the down arrow next to the Reply button and then selecting Reply to All.

Forward Messages

You can also forward an existing message to another party.

1. In the original message, click the down arrow next to the Reply button and then click Forward. This expands the message to include a forward box.

2. Add the recipient's email address in the To box.

3. Enter your own message into the main message box.

4. Click the Send button to send the message.

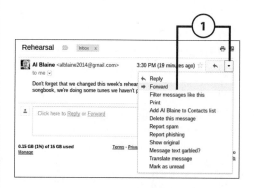

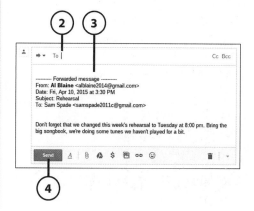

Sending New Messages

It's easy to compose and send new messages with Gmail. When you need to, you can attach one or more files to a message. You also can add a signature to your messages.

Compose a New Message

New messages you send are composed in a New Message pane that appears at the bottom-right corner of the Gmail window.

1. Click the Compose button at the top of the left column on any Gmail page. This opens a New Message pane.

2. Enter the recipient's email address in the To box. Gmail will suggest recipients from your contacts list; choose one of these suggestions or continue typing the address. Separate multiple recipients with commas.

3. Enter a subject for the message into the Subject box.

4. Enter the text of your message in the large text box. Click the Formatting Options button at the bottom of the pane to enhance your text with bold, italic, and other formats.

5. When you're done composing your message, click the Send button.

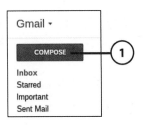

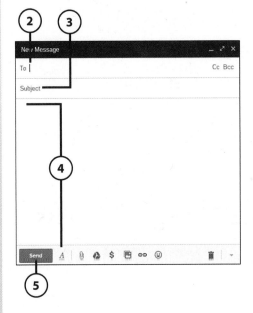

Spell Checking

Gmail includes a built-in spell checker. Any potentially misspelled words are identified with a squiggly red underline. Right-click a word to see a list of suggested spellings; click the correct spelling to fix the word.

>>>*Go Further*

CC AND BCC

You can also carbon copy and blind carbon copy additional recipients to a message. With a carbon copy (Cc), the original recipients see the new recipient. With a blind carbon copy (Bcc), the new recipient's name is hidden from the original recipients.

To add a Cc or Bcc, click either the Cc or Bcc link in the New Message pane. This expands the message to include a Cc or Bcc box, into which you enter the recipients' email addresses.

Attach a File to a Message

When you need to send a digital photo or other file to a friend or colleague, you can do so via email. To send a file via email, you attach that file to a standard email message. When the message is sent, the file attachment travels along with it; when the message is received, the file is right there, waiting to be opened.

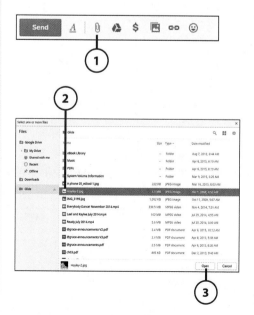

1. Compose a new message and then click the Attach Files (paperclip) button at the bottom of the New Message pane.

2. When the Files app opens, navigate to and select the file you want to attach.

3. Click the Open button.

4. The file you selected now appears at the bottom of the New Message pane. Continue to compose, and then send your message as normal.

Add a Signature to Your Messages

A *signature* is personalized text that appears at the bottom of an email message. Signatures typically include the sender's name and contact information, or some personal message. Gmail lets you create a single signature and apply it to all your outgoing email messages.

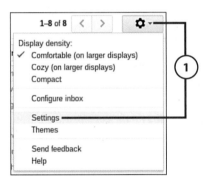

1. Click the Settings button; then click Settings to display the Gmail Settings page with the General tab selected.

2. Scroll down to the Signature section.

3. Enter your desired signature into the text box. This deselects the No Signature option.

4. Use the formatting controls to format your signature.

5. If you want to include your signature in the replies you make to email messages, click the Insert This Signature Before Quoted Text in Replies… option.

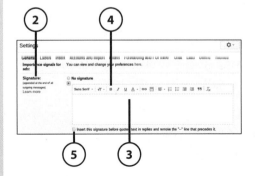

6. Scroll to the bottom of the page and click the Save Changes button. Your signature will now be automatically added to all new email messages you compose.

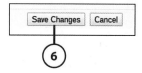

Managing Your Messages

When you receive a lot of messages in your inbox, the sheer number can become unwieldy. Fortunately, Gmail offers several ways to manage the messages you receive.

Assign Labels to a Message

Unlike other services, Gmail doesn't let you organize messages into folders. Instead, Gmail lets you "tag" messages with one or more labels. This has the effect of creating virtual folders, as you can search and sort your messages by any of the labels you create.

1. In the Gmail inbox, check those messages you want to share the same label.

2. Click the Labels button. Gmail displays a list of all existing labels.

3. Select a label from the list.

4. To create a new label, select Create New from the list.

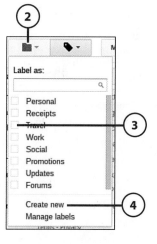

5. When the New Label dialog box appears, enter the name of the new label.

6. Click the Create button. Now the label you just created can be seen in the navigation pane. The messages you checked will appear when you click this newly created label.

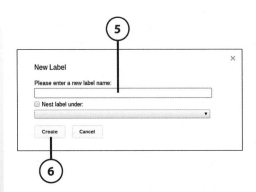

Multiple Labels

You can apply multiple labels to a single message. To apply another label to the same message(s), just repeat this procedure. After you assign a label, that label appears before the message's subject line.

Filter Messages by Label

After you've assigned labels to your messages, all of these labels appear in the Labels list. You can use this list to display only those messages that have a specific label.

1. In the Gmail inbox, scroll to the Labels list in the navigation pane.

2. Click the desired label. Gmail now displays all the messages designated with that label.

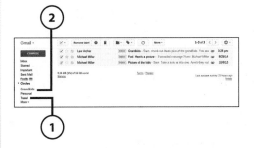

Star and Mark Important Messages

Gmail lets you mark selected messages as "important." Messages marked as important get displayed first in the Inbox. Gmail also learns from the messages you mark as important to flag similar messages the same way going forward.

In addition, you can *star* messages you want to come back to later. In effect, Gmail "starring" is the same as the "flagging" feature you find in competing email services and programs.

1. To mark a message in the Inbox as important, click the empty Important icon. The icon turns gold.

2. To star a message in the Inbox, click the empty star next to the message. The icon turns gold.

3. To display only important messages, click Important in the navigation pane.

4. To display only starred messages, click Starred in the navigation pane.

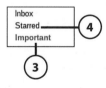

Search for Messages

Building on Google's search expertise, you can also search your Gmail inbox for messages that contain specific text or that are from a specific sender.

1. Enter your search query, in the form of one or more keywords, into the search box at the top of any Gmail page.

2. Click the Search button or press Enter.

3. Gmail now returns a search results page. This page lists messages in which the keywords you entered appear anywhere in the email—in the subject line, in the message text, or in the sender or recipient lists. Click a message to read it.

Delete Messages

You can easily delete one or more messages at a time from the Inbox.

1. From the Gmail inbox, check those messages you want to delete.

2. Click the Delete button, or press the Delete key on your Chromebook keyboard.

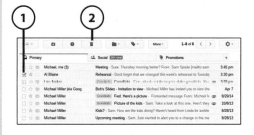

Editing a letter with Google Docs

In this chapter, you learn how to use the Google Docs word processing app.

→ Getting to Know Google Docs
→ Working with Documents
→ Editing Documents
→ Formatting Documents
→ Printing and Sharing Documents

Word Processing with Google Docs

If you do any productivity work at all, you're familiar with Microsoft Office, Microsoft's suite of productivity applications. This suite—which includes the Microsoft Word word processor, Microsoft Excel spreadsheet program, and Microsoft PowerPoint presentation program—consists of traditional software-based applications, and therefore can't be run on your cloud-based Chromebook.

Fortunately, a number of web-based productivity apps are available, the most popular of which is Google's own Google Docs suite. The word processor in this suite is also called Google Docs, and it works a lot like Microsoft Word—except that it runs in your web browser, over the Internet. (It's also free, which is another marked difference from the Microsoft Office apps.)

As a web-based app, Google Docs itself and all the documents you create with it are not stored locally on your computer, but rather on the Internet, in the so-called cloud. This means you can use Google

Docs on your Chromebook wherever you have an Internet connection—and on any other computer, smartphone, or tablet with an Internet connection. You can also share your Google Docs documents with other users, which is great for group collaboration.

Getting to Know Google Docs

The Google Docs word processor is just one part of the Google Docs suite. The other components are Google Sheets (spreadsheets) and Google Slides (presentations). All three apps are compatible with files created in their Microsoft Office counterparts; Docs can read and write Microsoft Word files, Sheets can read and write Microsoft Excel files, and Slides can read and write Microsoft PowerPoint files.

Navigate the Google Docs Dashboard

You access Google Docs in the Chrome browser, by launching the Google Docs app from Chrome's Apps panel or on the desktop Shelf. This opens the Docs dashboard in a Chrome browser window.

Open File Picker

Previously created documents

Sort Options

Menu button

List View/Grid View

Click to create new document

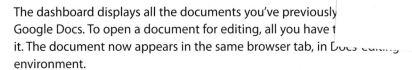

The dashboard displays all the documents you've previously
Google Docs. To open a document for editing, all you have t
it. The document now appears in the same browser tab, in Docs editing
environment.

Along the top of the Docs dashboard is a blue toolbar. Click the Menu button
on the left to switch to the Sheets or Slides dashboard, or to adjust general
settings. Click the List View or Grid View button to switch to List or Grid View.
Click the Sort Options button to sort the files by title, last edited, last opened,
or last modified. Click the File Picker button to find other files to open.

Navigate the Google Docs Editor

When you open an existing document or create a new document, you see
the Docs word processor in editing mode. It looks a lot like Microsoft Word—
or at least an older version of Word, before it went to the "ribbon" interface.
You have a big blank space to create your document, a pull-down menu bar,
and a toolbar with common commands. It's pretty familiar looking and fairly
easy to use.

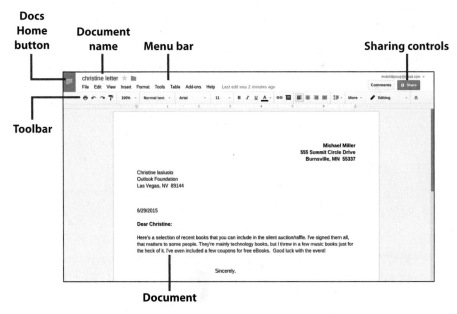

That said, Google Docs doesn't include all the functionality you're used to in
Microsoft Word. In particular, Docs lacks some of Word's more sophisticated
document formatting. But Google Docs is a decent replacement for Word

if your needs are fairly traditional; it should do for the majority of everyday users. Put simply, it's the best cloud-based word processor for use with your Chromebook.

Working with Documents

Google Docs makes it easy to create new documents and open existing documents. You can even import documents from Microsoft Word, or export your documents into Microsoft Word format.

Open an Existing Document

You access all your existing documents from the Docs dashboard.

1. Click the Google Docs icon on the Shelf to open the Google Docs app.

2. Click the document you want to open.

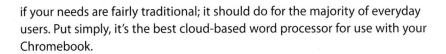

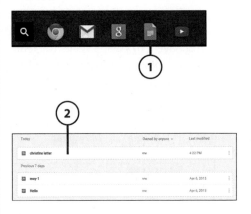

Create a New Document

You create new documents from the Google Docs dashboard, as well.

1. In the Google Docs dashboard, click the blue + button at the lower right.

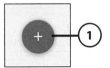

2. A new blank document opens in the same browser tab. To name this document, click Untitled Document at the top of the page, just above the menu bar.

3. Docs displays the Rename Document dialog box. Enter the title for your new document.

4. Click OK to return to your document and start editing.

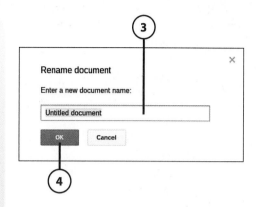

Saving Your Document

It's easy to save a document in Google Docs—in fact, you don't have to do anything. That's because Docs automatically saves all documents you're working on to your Google Drive online. Any time you make a change to the document, the document is automatically saved again. There is nothing you have to do manually.

Import a Word Document

If you work with colleagues who use Microsoft Word, you can use Google Docs to view and edit the documents that Word creates.

1. From the Docs dashboard, click the File Picker button to open the File Picker.

2. If the document is stored on Google Drive, click My Drive.

3. Click the file you want to import.

4. Click the Select button to import the file.

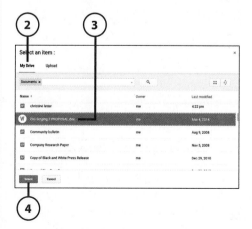

5. If the document is stored on your Chromebook or on an external storage device, click Upload.

6. Click Select a File from Your Computer to open the Files app.

7. When the Files app opens, click the file you want to import.

8. Click the Open button. The document now opens in Google Docs for editing.

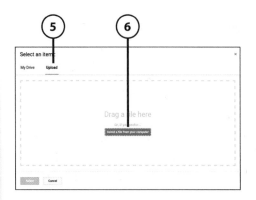

Export a Document to Word

Any Google Docs document you create can be downloaded in Microsoft Word format for viewing and editing by anyone using Word.

1. From within the document you wish to export, click the File menu.

2. Click Download As.

3. Click Microsoft Word (.docx).

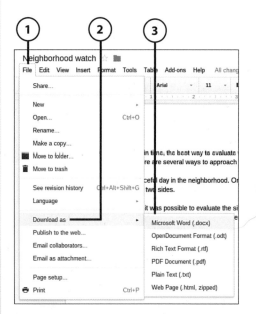

4. When the Files app opens, select Google Drive to save to your Google Drive, Downloads to save on your Chromebook, or any attached external storage device to save there.

5. Accept or edit the suggested file name in the File Name box.

6. Click the Save button.

Editing Documents

Google Docs' editing functions are very similar to those in Microsoft Word. If you know how to use Word, you don't have to learn much new.

Enter Text

If you can type, you can add new text to a Docs document.

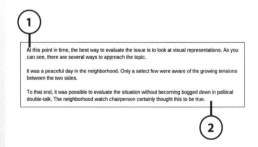

1. Use your mouse or the keyboard's arrow keys to position the cursor where you want to enter the new text.

2. Start typing.

Copy and Paste Text

On occasion, you may find it helpful to copy an existing word or block of text to another point in the document. You do this with Docs' Copy and Paste commands.

1. Use your mouse to select the text you want to copy.

Selecting with the Keyboard

You can also select text with the keyboard. Move the cursor to where you want the selection to begin, press and hold the Shift key, and then use the arrow keys to move to the end of the selection.

2. Click Edit, Copy or press Ctrl+C.

3. Move the cursor to where you want to copy the text.

4. Click Edit, Paste or press Ctrl+V.

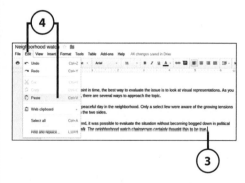

Move Text

You can also move text from one place in a document to another location, using the Cut and Paste commands. When you cut and paste text, it moves from one location to another. (When you copy text, as discussed previously, the original version remains in place and a copy is placed in a different location.)

1. Use your mouse or keyboard to select the text you want to move.

2. Click Edit, Cut or press Ctrl+X.

3. Move the cursor to where you want to move the text.

4. Click Edit, Paste or press Ctrl+V.

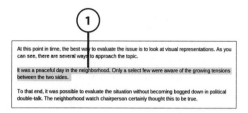

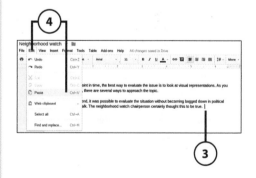

Check Your Spelling

When you type, you may introduce spelling errors into your text. Fortunately, Google Docs includes a spell checker for your use.

1. Words that are potentially misspelled are identified with a squiggly red underline. Right-click the misspelled word.

2. Docs offers a selection of corrections. If the correct spelling is listed, click it to replace the original word with the new one.

3. If the selected word is not mis-spelled but simply not known to Docs' spell checker, click Add to Personal Dictionary.

4. To force the spell checker to ignore all instances of the identi-fied word, click Ignore All.

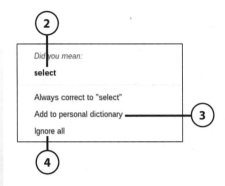

Formatting Documents

Google Docs offers a variety of formatting options for the documents you create. You can format individual words or blocks of text, as well as complete paragraphs.

Format Text

You can format the font, font size, font color, and other characteristics of selected text.

1. Use your mouse or keyboard to select the text you want to format.

2. To change the text font, click Font on the toolbar and make a new selection.

3. To change the size of the font, click Font Size on the toolbar and make a new selection.

4. To bold the selected text, click the Bold button or press Ctrl+B.

5. To italicize the selected text, click the Italic button or press Ctrl+I.

6. To underline the selected text, click the Underline button or press Ctrl+U.

7. To change the color of the text, click the Text Color button and make a new selection.

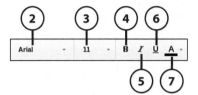

Format a Paragraph

Certain formatting options, such as alignment and line spacing, apply to an entire paragraph.

1. Use your mouse or keyboard to position the cursor anywhere in the paragraph you want to format.

2. To change the paragraph alignment, click either the Left Align, Center Align, Right Align, or Justify button on the toolbar.

3. To change the spacing between lines, click the Line Spacing button and make a new selection.

4. To turn the paragraph into a numbered or bulleted list, click the More button and then make a selection.

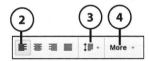

Apply Styles

Google Docs includes several pre-designed styles that you can apply to selected paragraphs. These styles include font, font size, and other formatting options. For example, the Title style formats text properly for use as a document title; the Normal Text style is best for normal body text.

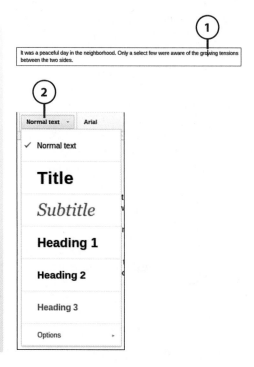

1. Use your mouse or keyboard to position the cursor anywhere in the paragraph you want to format.

2. Click the Styles button on the toolbar and make a selection. The paragraph is formatted with the selected style.

Printing and Sharing Documents

You have a number of ways to share a document you create in Google Docs, including printing a hard copy and sharing online, via the Web.

Print a Document

Printing within Google Docs is handled by Google's Cloud Print service—which means you have to have Cloud Print configured before you start to print. (Learn more in Chapter 18, "Printing with Google Cloud Print.")

1. From within the document you want to print, click the Print button on the toolbar.

2. This opens a Google Cloud Print panel. If the Destination setting is not the printer you want, click the Change button and select a different printer.

3. By default, the entire document will print, but if you only want to print part of a document, go to the Pages section and enter a specific page or range of pages into the text box.

4. Click the Print button.

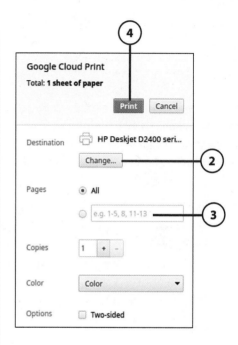

Share a Document with Others

Sharing a Google Docs document is similar to sharing any file on Google Drive. You have the option of letting others only view the shared document or edit it—the latter of which is what you want if you're collaborating on a group project.

1. From within the document you want to share, click the Share button to display the Share with Others pane.

2. Enter the names or email addresses of the people you want to share this document with into the People box. Separate multiple names or email addresses with commas.

3. Click the button to the right of the People box and select whether these people Can Edit, Can Comment, or Can View this document.

4. Click the Send button, and the document is shared with those selected people.

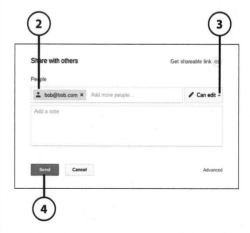

>>>Go Further

USING GOOGLE DOCS OFFLINE

Although Google Docs is a web-based application—which means you need to be connected to the Internet to run it—it does have a special offline mode you can use when you don't have an Internet connection handy. In Docs' offline mode, you pre-download your documents so you can work without a connection, and then you synchronize ("sync") your work to Google Drive the next time you're connected.

To enable offline access for Docs, Sheets, and Slides, go to any of the Docs dashboards, click the Menu button, and then select Settings. When the Settings dialog box appears, click Turn On in the Offline Sync section; then click OK. All of your Docs, Sheets, and Slides files will now be synced so that they're available when you don't have an Internet connection.

To use Google Docs offline, just launch the Docs, Sheets, or Slides app, open a file, and start working. The next time you connect to the Internet, the changes you've made will automatically be synchronized with the versions of those files stored online in Google Drive. You don't have to do anything, manually, to make this happen—it all occurs in the background.

Editing a spreadsheet with Google Sheets

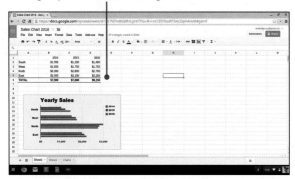

In this chapter, you learn how to use the Google Sheets spreadsheet app.

→ Getting to Know Google Sheets
→ Working with Spreadsheets
→ Entering and Editing Data
→ Formatting Cells and Data
→ Working with Formulas and Functions
→ Creating Charts
→ Printing and Sharing Spreadsheets

Spreadsheets with Google Sheets

Just as Google Docs resembles a web-based version of the Microsoft Word word processor, Google Sheets is a web-based spreadsheet app that works much like Microsoft Excel. You use Sheets to work with numbers—including writing complex formulas and using predefined functions.

Getting to Know Google Sheets

The Google Sheets spreadsheet application is just one part of the Google Docs suite. You learned about the Google Docs word processor in the previous chapter; you'll learn about the Google Slides presentation app in the next chapter.

Navigate the Google Sheets Dashboard

You access Google Sheets in the Chrome browser, by launching the Google Sheets app from Chrome's Apps panel. This opens the Sheets dashboard in a Chrome browser window.

Sort Options

Open File Picker

Menu button

List View/ Grid View

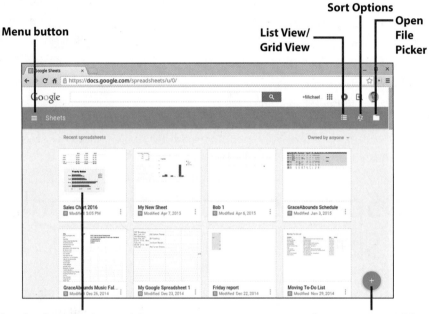

Previously created spreadsheets

Create new spreadsheet

The dashboard displays all the spreadsheets you've previously created with Google Sheets. To open a spreadsheet file for editing, all you have to do is click it. The spreadsheet now appears in the same browser tab, in Sheets' editing environment.

Along the top of the Sheets dashboard is a green toolbar. Click the Menu button on the left to switch to the Docs or Slides dashboard, or to adjust general settings. Click the List View or Grid View buttons to switch to List or Grid View. Click the Sort Options button to sort the files by title, last edited, last opened, or last modified. Click the File Picker button to find other files to open.

Navigate Google Sheets

When you open an existing spreadsheet or create a new spreadsheet, you see the Sheets app in editing mode. It looks a lot like Microsoft Excel, but with traditional pull-down menus instead of Excel's newer "ribbon" interface. At the top of the window you see a pull-down menu bar and a toolbar with common commands. The spreadsheet itself is in the middle of the window, with rows and columns defining individual cells. At the bottom of the window is a series of tabs (just one appears by default); click a tab to switch to a different sheet within the main spreadsheet file.

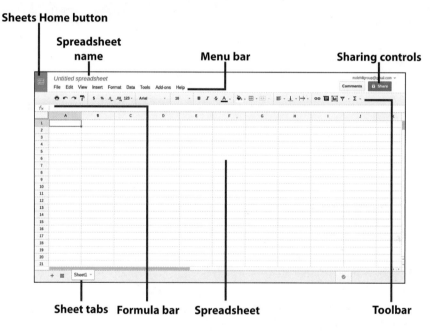

Sheets Home button

Spreadsheet name

Menu bar

Sharing controls

Sheet tabs   Formula bar   Spreadsheet   Toolbar

Working with Spreadsheets

Google Sheets makes it easy to create new spreadsheets and open existing spreadsheets. You can even import files from Microsoft Excel, or export your spreadsheets into Microsoft Excel format.

Open an Existing Spreadsheet

You access all your existing spreadsheet files from the Sheets dashboard.

1. Open the Apps panel.

2. Click the Google Sheets icon to open the Google Sheets app.

3. Click the spreadsheet you want to open.

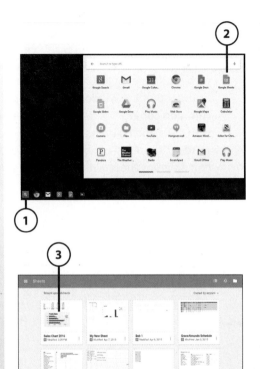

Create a New Spreadsheet

You also create new spreadsheets from the Google Sheets dashboard.

1. In the Google Sheets dashboard, click the green + button at the lower right.

2. A new blank spreadsheet opens in the same browser tab. To name this spreadsheet, click Untitled Spreadsheet at the top of the page to display the Rename Spreadsheet dialog box.

3. Enter the title for your new document.

4. Click OK.

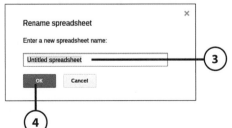

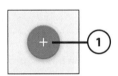

Saving Your Spreadsheet

It's easy to save a spreadsheet file in Google Sheets—in fact, you don't have to do anything. That's because Sheets automatically saves all files you're working on to your Google Drive online. Any time you make a change to the spreadsheet, the file is automatically saved again. There is nothing you have to do manually.

Import an Excel File

If you work with colleagues who use Microsoft Excel, you can use Google Sheets to view and edit the spreadsheets that Excel creates.

1. From the Sheets dashboard, click the File Picker button to open the File Picker.

2. If the spreadsheet file is stored on Google Drive, click My Drive.

3. Click the file you want to import.

4. Click the Select button to import the file.

5. If the spreadsheet file is stored on your Chromebook or on an external storage device, click Upload.

6. Click Select a File from Your Computer to open the Files app.

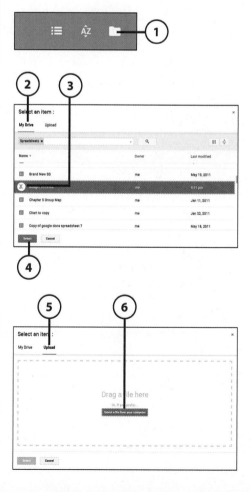

7. Click the file you want to open.

8. Click the Open button. The spreadsheet now opens in Google Sheets for editing.

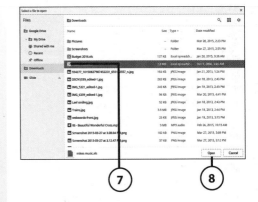

Export a Spreadsheet to Excel

Any Google Sheets spreadsheet you create can be downloaded in Microsoft Excel format for viewing and editing by anyone using Excel.

1. From within the spreadsheet you wish to export, click the File menu.

2. Click Download As.

3. Click Microsoft Excel (.xlsx).

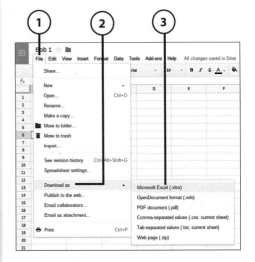

4. When the Files app opens, select Google Drive to save to your Google Drive, Downloads to save on your Chromebook, or any attached external storage device to save there.

5. Accept or edit the suggested file name in the File Name box.

6. Click the Save button.

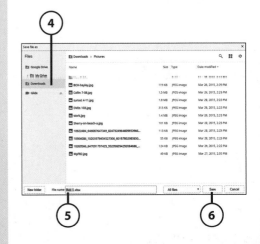

Entering and Editing Data

Google Sheets' data entering and editing functions are very similar to those in Microsoft Excel. If you know how to use Excel, you don't have to learn much new.

Enter Data

If you can type, you can add new data to a spreadsheet.

1. Use your mouse or the keyboard's arrow keys to move to the cell where you want to enter data.

2. Start typing.

3. Press Enter when done to close the cell for editing.

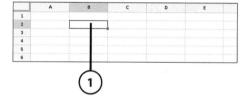

Edit Cell Data

If you need to correct or change the data in an existing cell, it's easy to do.

1. Use your mouse or keyboard to select the cell you wish to edit.

2. The contents of the selected cell are mirrored in the Formula bar. Click here and edit the contents of the cell.

3. Press Enter to register your changes.

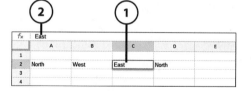

Select Rows and Columns

You select an individual cell by moving to it with your mouse or keyboard. You can also select entire rows and columns for editing or formatting.

1. To select an entire row, click the row header on the left.

2. To select an entire column, click the column header above.

	A	B	C	D	E
1					
2	North	West	East	North	
3	12	22	4	13	
4	13	21	2	12	
5	14	24	6	14	
6	15	23	8	13	
7					
8					

Rows, Columns, and Cells

Rows are horizontal and are identified by numbers. Columns are vertical and are identified by letters. An individual cell is identified by the column letter and row number that intersect at that cell. For example, the cell in the first row and first column is labeled cell A1.

	A	B	C	D
1				
2	North	West	East	North
3	12	22	4	13
4	13	21	2	12
5	14	24	6	14
6	15	23	8	13
7				
8				
9				

Work with Sheets and Tabs

A spreadsheet file can contain multiple sheets, each on its own tab. This way you can include related data in the same spreadsheet file.

1. To create a new tab, click the + button at the bottom of the current sheet.

2. To rename a sheet, double-click it, type a new name, and then press Enter.

3. To switch to a different sheet, click that sheet's tab.

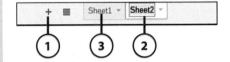

Formatting Cells and Data

Google Sheets lets you format the data within cells—change the font, color, and so forth—as well as the cells themselves.

Format Cell Data

You can format the font, font size, font color, and other characteristics of the text and numbers within a cell.

1. Use your mouse or keyboard to select the cell or cells you want to format.

2. To change the font, click the Font button on the toolbar and make a new selection.

3. To change the size of the font, click the Font Size button on the toolbar and make a new selection.

4. To bold the selection, click the Bold button or press Ctrl+B.

5. To italicize the selection, click the Italic button or press Ctrl+I.

6. To strike through the selection, click the Strikethrough button.

7. To change the color of the data, click the Text Color button and make a new selection.

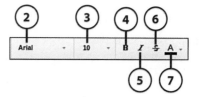

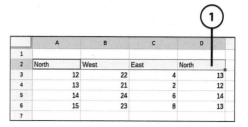

Format Numbers

You have a number of ways to format the numbers you enter into a cell. The Number format uses a comma to separate thousands, and it displays two decimal places. The Percent format expresses the number as a percent with two decimal places. The Currency format adds a dollar sign and also displays two decimal places. And there are more formats than those available.

1. Use your mouse or keyboard to select the cell or cells you want to format. By default, numbers are formatted with the Automatic format.

2. To apply the Currency format, click the Format as Currency button.

3. To apply the Percent format, click the Format as Percent button.

4. To apply other number formats, click the More Formats button and make a selection.

5. To decrease the number of decimal places displayed, click the Decrease Decimal Places button.

6. To increase the number of deci mal places displayed, click the Increase Decimal Places button.

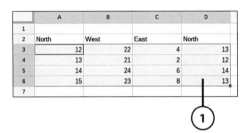

Format Cell Color

One way to distinguish different cells or types of data in a spreadsheet is to change the background color of those cells.

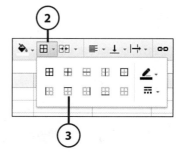

1. Use your mouse or keyboard to select the cell or cells you want to format.

2. Click the Fill Color button to display the color picker.

3. Click the color you want.

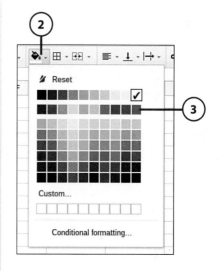

Format Cell Borders

You can also apply different types of borders to selected cells. For example, you can surround a group of cells with a full border, or apply top and bottom borders to a title or summary row.

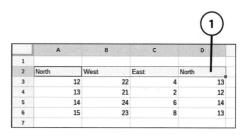

1. Use your mouse or keyboard to select the cell or cells you want to format.

2. Click the Borders button to display the available types of borders.

3. Click the border style you want to apply.

>>>Go Further
WORKING WITH RANGES

When you reference data within a spreadsheet, you can reference individual cells or you can reference a range of cells. When you reference more than one contiguous cell, that's called a *range*. You typically use ranges with specific functions, such as SUM (which totals a range of cells) or AVERAGE (which calculates the average value of a range of cells).

A range reference is expressed by listing the first and last cells in the range, separated by a colon (:). For example, the range that starts with cell A1 and ends with cell A9 is written like this:

A1:A9

You can select a range with either your mouse or your keyboard. Using your mouse, you can simply click and drag the cursor to select all the cells in the range. Using your keyboard, position the cursor in the first cell in the range, hold down the Shift key, and then use the cursor keys to expand the range in the appropriate direction.

Working with Formulas and Functions

After you've entered data into your spreadsheet, you need to work with those numbers to create other numbers. You do this as you would in the real world, by using common formulas to calculate your data by addition, subtraction, multiplication, and division. You can also use advanced formulas preprogrammed into Google Sheets; these advanced formulas are called *functions*.

Entering a Formula

A formula can consist of numbers, mathematical operators, and the contents of other cells (referred to by the cell reference). You construct a formula from the following elements:

- An equals sign (=). This = sign is necessary at the start of each formula.
- One or more specific numbers.

and/or

- One or more cell references.
- A mathematical operator (such as + or –). This is needed if your formula contains more than one cell reference or number.

For example, to add the contents of cells A1 and A2, you enter this formula:

=A1+A2

The most common operators are + (add), – (subtract), * (multiply), and / (divide).

1. Select the cell that will contain the formula.

2. Type = to start the formula.

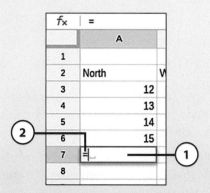

3. Enter the rest of the formula. Remember to refer to specific cells by the "A1, B1, etc." cell reference. Cells that you reference in the formula appear in dashed colored outline.

4. Press Enter to accept the formula. You now see the results of the formula in the cell. The formula itself is visible in the Formula bar above the spreadsheet.

f_x	=A3+A4+A5+A6
	A
1	
2	North We
3	12
4	13
5	14
6	15
7	54
8	

④

Using Functions

A function is a type of formula built in to Google Sheets. You can use these built-in functions instead of writing complex formulas in your spreadsheets; you can also include functions as part of your formulas.

For example, if you want to total the values in cells B4 through B7, you could create a formula to add each cell individually. Or you could use the SUM function, which lets you total (sum) a column or row of numbers without having to type every cell into the formula, like this:

=sum(B4:B7)

Google Sheets uses most of the same functions as those used in Microsoft Excel. All functions use the following format:

=function(argument)

Replace function with the name of the function, and replace argument with a range reference. The argument always appears in parentheses.

You can enter a function into a formula either by typing the name of the function or by clicking the Functions button on the toolbar and then selecting a function.

1. Select the cell that will contain the result of the function.

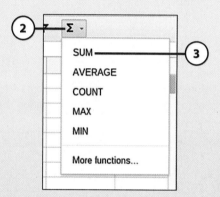

2. Click the Functions button on the toolbar.

3. The five most common functions (SUM, AVERAGE, COUNT, MAX, and MIN) are listed here. Click to use one of these functions.

4. The function is now entered into the selected cell. Enter the necessary cell references (or select the referenced cells) for this function.

5. Press Enter to complete the function. You now see the result of the function in the cell. The function itself is visible in the Formula bar above the spreadsheet when you select the cell that contains the formula result.

fx	=SUM(D3:D6)			
	A	B	C	D
1				
2	North	West	East	North
3	12	22	4	13
4	13	21	2	12
5	14	24	6	14
6	15	23	8	13
7	54			52
8				

5

More Functions

To view all the functions available in Google Sheets, click the Functions button and then select More Functions. This opens a new browser tab and displays the Google Spreadsheets Function List. Use the information here to enter and use specific functions in your spreadsheet.

Creating Charts

Some data is best represented visually. To that end, Google Sheets enables you to create colorful charts out of the data in your spreadsheets.

Create a Basic Chart

Google Sheets offers several types of popular charts, including line, area, column, bar, scatter, pie, map, and trend charts. Each type of chart is available in several different variations; choose the chart type that best represents your specific data.

1. Use your keyboard or mouse to select the cells that contain the data you want to chart. Make sure you include any heading rows or columns.

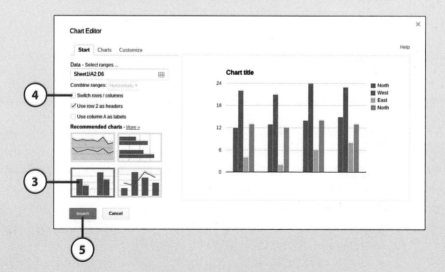

	A	B	C	D
1				
2	North	West	East	North
3	12	22	4	13
4	13	21	2	12
5	14	24	6	14
6	15	23	8	13
7				

2. Click the Insert Chart button on the toolbar. This displays the Chart Editor pane, with the Start tab selected.

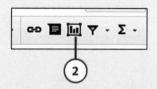

3. In most instances, you will want to use one of the recommended charts on the Start tab. Click the chart type you want; you see a preview of the chart on the right side of the pane.

4. If you need to switch rows and columns in the chart, check the Switch Rows/Columns option.

5. If you like what you see, click the Insert button. The chart is now inserted in your spreadsheet.

Select a Different Chart Type

In some instances, Sheets' recommended chart types aren't what you actually want to use. Fortunately, Sheets lets you apply other chart types to your data.

1. From within the Chart Editor, select the Charts tab.

2. Click the type of chart you want from the left column.

3. Click the specific variation from the thumbnails presented.

4. Click the Insert button. The chart is now inserted in your spreadsheet.

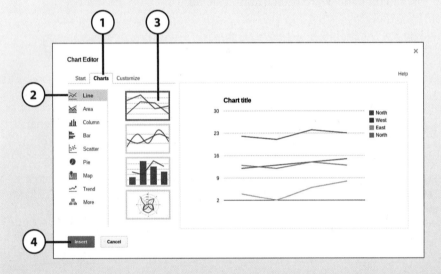

Customize a Chart

Once you create a chart, you can customize its placement and its look and feel.

1. Click to select the chart.

2. To move the chart elsewhere on the spreadsheet, click at the top of the chart and then click and drag it to the new position.

3. To resize the chart, click and drag one of the bottom corners until the chart is sized appropriately.

4. To edit any element within the chart, click that element and then make your changes.

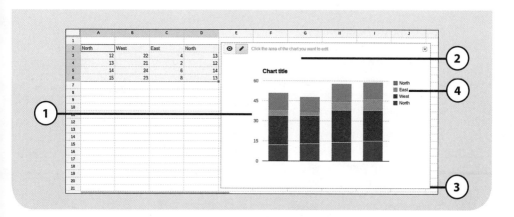

Printing and Sharing Spreadsheets

You have a number of ways to share a spreadsheet you create in Google Sheets, including printing a hard copy and sharing online, via the Web.

Print a Spreadsheet

Printing within Google Sheets is handled by Google's Cloud Print service—which means you have to have Cloud Print configured before you start to print. (Learn more in Chapter 18, "Printing with Google Cloud Print.")

1. From within the spreadsheet you want to print, click the Print button on the toolbar. This opens the Print Settings panel.

2. To print just the current sheet, select Current Sheet.

3. To print all sheets in the spreadsheet, select All Sheets.

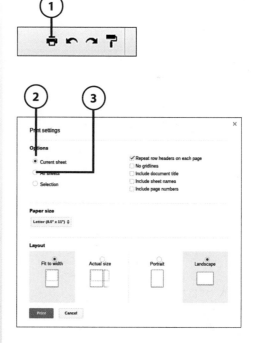

4. By default, row headers are displayed on every page of a multiple-page printout. To *not* display row headers on each page, uncheck the option Repeat Row Headers on Each Page.

5. To fit the spreadsheet contents to the width of a single page, select the Fit to Width option. Otherwise, select Actual Size.

6. To select the page layout, select either Portrait or Landscape.

7. Click the Print button. This opens the Google Cloud Print panel.

8. If the Destination setting is not the printer you want, click the Change button and select a different printer.

9. If you only want to print part of a spreadsheet, go to the Pages section and enter a specific page or range of pages into the text box.

10. Click the Print button.

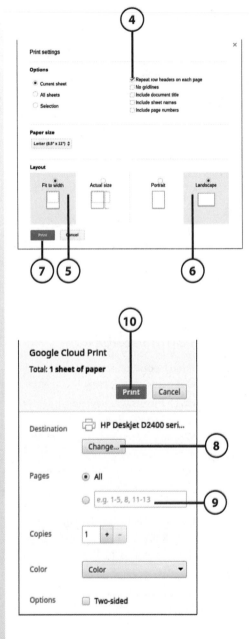

Share a Spreadsheet with Others

Sharing a Google Sheets spreadsheet is similar to sharing any file on Google Drive. You have the option of letting others only view the shared spreadsheet or edit it—the latter of which is what you want if you're collaborating on a group project.

1. From within the spreadsheet you want to share, click the Share button to display the Share with Others pane.

2. Enter the names or email addresses of the people you want to share this document with into the People box. Separate multiple names or email addresses with commas.

3. Click the button to the right of the People box and select whether these people Can Edit, Can Comment, or Can View this spreadsheet.

4. Click the Send button, and the spreadsheet is shared with those selected people.

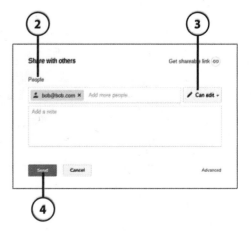

Editing a presentation with Google Slides

In this chapter, you learn how to create presentations with Google Slides.

→ Getting to Know Google Slides
→ Working with Presentations
→ Managing the Slides in Your Presentation
→ Working with Text and Graphics
→ Changing the Look and Feel of a Presentation
→ Using Transitions and Animations
→ Giving Live Presentations
→ Printing and Sharing Presentations

Presentations with Google Slides

Google Slides is Google's presentation app, similar in functionality to Microsoft PowerPoint. You use Google Slides to create and give onscreen presentations—either in person or over the Internet.

Getting to Know Google Slides

The Google Slides presentation application is just one part of the Google Docs suite. You learned about the Google Docs word processor and Google Sheets spreadsheet in previous chapters.

Navigate the Google Slides Dashboard

You access Google Slides in the Chrome browser, by launching the Google Slides app from Chrome's Apps panel. This opens the Slides dashboard in a Chrome browser window.

The dashboard displays all the presentations you've previously created with Google Slides. To open a presentation for editing, all you have to do is click it. The presentation now appears in the same browser tab, in Slides' editing environment.

Along the top of the Slides dashboard is a yellow toolbar. Click the Menu button on the left to switch to the Docs or Sheets dashboard, or to adjust general settings. Click the List View or Grid View button to switch to List or Grid View. Click the Sort Options button to sort the files by title, last edited, last opened, or last modified. Click the File Picker button to find other files to open.

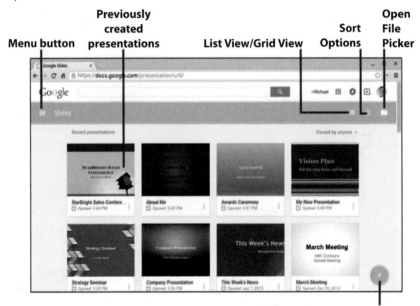

Previously created presentations

Menu button

List View/Grid View

Sort Options

Open File Picker

Create new presentation

Navigate Google Slides

When you open an existing presentation or create a new presentation, you see the Slides app in editing mode. It looks a lot like Microsoft PowerPoint, but with traditional pull-down menus instead of PowerPoint's newer "ribbon" interface. At the top of the window you see a pull-down menu bar and a toolbar with common commands. The left side of the window is the slide sorter, which displays all the slides in your presentation. The currently selected slide is displayed in the slide editor on the right, ready for editing. Below the slide editor is a space for speaker notes for the current slide.

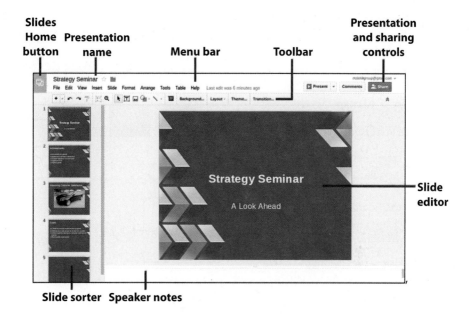

Slides Home button — **Presentation name** — **Menu bar** — **Toolbar** — **Presentation and sharing controls** — **Slide editor**

Slide sorter — **Speaker notes**

Working with Presentations

Google Slides makes it easy to create new presentations and open existing presentations. You can even import presentations from Microsoft PowerPoint, or export your presentations into Microsoft PowerPoint format.

Open an Existing Presentation

You access all your existing presentation files from the Slides dashboard.

1. Open the Apps panel.

2. Click the Google Slides icon to open the Google Slides app.

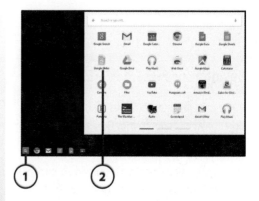

3. Click the presentation you want to open.

Create a New Presentation

You also create new presentations from the Google Slides dashboard.

1. In the Google Slides dashboard, click the yellow + button at the lower right.

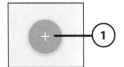

2. You now see the Choose a Theme pane. Click the theme you want to use, or click Cancel to create your presentation without a visual theme.

3. Click OK. The presentation opens with one blank slide displayed.

4. To name this presentation, click Untitled Presentation to display the Rename Presentation dialog box.

5. Enter the title for your new presentation.

6. Click OK.

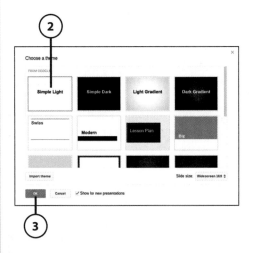

Saving Your Presentation

It's easy to save a presentation file in Google Slides—in fact, you don't have to do anything. That's because Slides automatically saves all files you're working on, to your Google Drive online. Any time you make a change to the presentation, the file is automatically saved again. There is nothing you have to do manually.

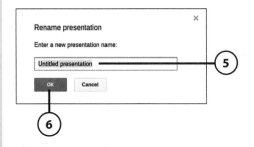

Import a PowerPoint File

If you work with colleagues who use Microsoft PowerPoint, you can use Google Slides to view and edit the presentations that PowerPoint creates.

1. From the Slides dashboard, click the File Picker button to open the File Picker.

2. If the presentation file is stored on Google Drive, click My Drive.

3. Click the file you want to import.

4. Click the Select button to import the file.

5. If the presentation file is stored on your Chromebook or on an external storage device, click Upload.

6. Click Select a File from Your Computer to display the Files app.

7. Navigate to and select the file you want to open.

8. Click the Open button. The presentation now opens in Google Slides for editing.

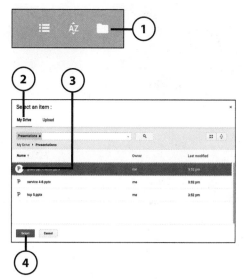

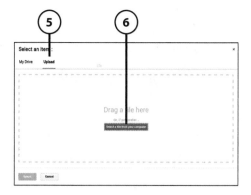

It's Not All Good

Compatibility Issues

Google Slides is not 100% compatible with Microsoft PowerPoint. Although Slides can read and write PowerPoint files, not all of PowerPoint's formatting, animations, and transitions translate. You may find that you need to do some reformatting and editing of a PowerPoint file you import.

>>>Go Further

POWERPOINT PRESENTATIONS IN GOOGLE SLIDES

Because PowerPoint is more fully featured than Google Slides, many users prefer to use PowerPoint to create their presentations. However, even if you continue to use PowerPoint to create and edit your presentations, you can use Google Slides to give those presentations when you're on the road. Just import your PowerPoint presentation into Google Slides, and then you can access that presentation from any computer connected to the Internet. There's no longer any need to take large PowerPoint files (or even your own notebook PC) with you when you travel!

Export a Presentation to PowerPoint

Any Google Slides presentation you create can be downloaded in Microsoft PowerPoint format, for viewing and editing by anyone using PowerPoint.

1. From within the presentation you wish to export, click the File menu.

2. Click Download As.

3. Click Microsoft PowerPoint (.pptx).

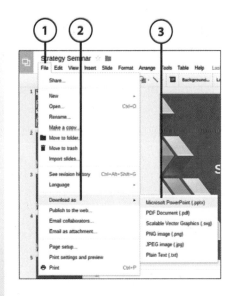

4. When the Files app opens, select Google Drive to save to your Google Drive, Downloads to save on your Chromebook, or any attached external storage device to save there.

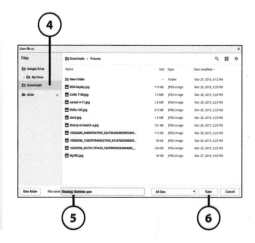

5. Accept or edit the suggested file name in the File Name box.

6. Click the Save button.

Managing the Slides in Your Presentation

In Google Slides, a slide can be based on one of six predesigned layouts:

- **Title Slide**—The slide consists of the presentation title and subtitle only (ideal for the lead slide in a presentation, or to signal new sections in the presentation).

- **Title and Body**—The slide consists of the slide title and a block of text below.

- **Title and Two Columns**—The slide consists of the slide title and two columns of text.

- **Title Only**—The slide consists of the slide title and then blank space below.

- **Caption**—The slide has no title or body text but only a caption at the bottom (ideal for big images or videos).

- **Blank**—The slide is completely blank. You can insert anything on this type of slide.

Choose the right layout for the information on each slide in your presentation.

Add a New Slide

Every new presentation starts with a single slide formatted as a Title Slide. You add new slides to create a complete presentation.

1. In the slide sorter pane, click the slide after which you want the new slide to appear.

2. Click the down arrow next to the New Slide (+) button on the toolbar.

3. Click the slide layout you want. The new slide appears, with the selected layout.

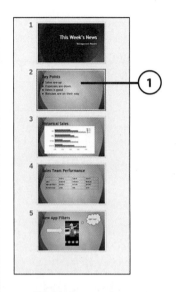

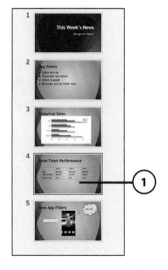

Delete a Slide

Of course, you don't always want to keep every slide you create. You may need to delete some slides from your presentation.

1. In the slide sorter pane, click the slide you want to delete.

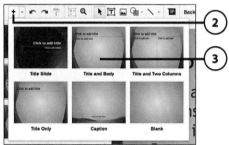

2. Click the File menu.

3. Click Move to Trash. Alternatively, you can just press the Delete key on your Chromebook keyboard.

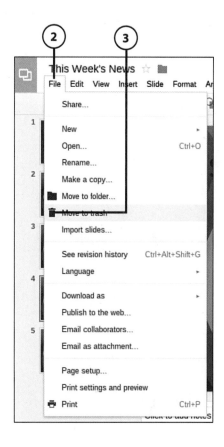

Rearrange Slides

As your presentation develops, you may need to rethink the order of the slides in the presentation. You rearrange your slides in the slide sorter, using your Chromebook's touchpad.

1. In the slide sorter pane, select the slide you want to move.

2. Click and drag the slide up or down to a new position.

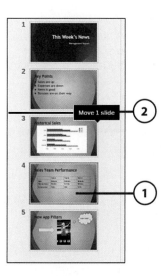

Working with Text and Graphics

Once you've chosen a slide layout, it's time to start adding content to that slide. Slide content can be in the form of text or images of various types.

Add and Format Text

Each block of text on a slide is added via a separate text object. Select an object to add, edit, or format the text within.

1. Click to select any text object, such as Click to Add Title or Click to Add Text.

2. Type the text into the text object.

3. Select any text you want to format.

4. Click the appropriate formatting controls (font, font size, bold, italic, etc.) in the toolbar to apply that formatting.

Web Links

To add a web page link to the text on a slide, select the anchor text and click the Insert Link button on the toolbar. When the link panel appears, paste or enter the web address (URL) for the linked-to page and then click Apply.

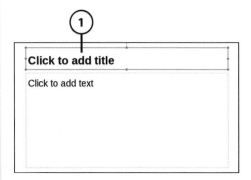

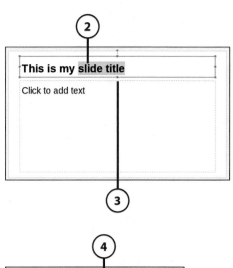

Add Images

Text isn't the only type of object you can add to a slide. Oftentimes you'll want to show a picture of some item on a slide, or just add graphics for visual interest.

1. Position the cursor where you want the image to appear.

2. Click the Image button on the toolbar to display the Insert Image panel.

3. Make sure the Upload tab is selected and then click Choose an Image to Upload.

4. When the Files app appears, select the image you want.

5. Click Open.

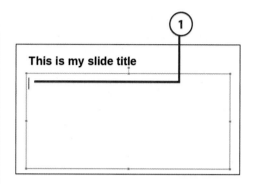

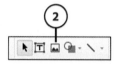

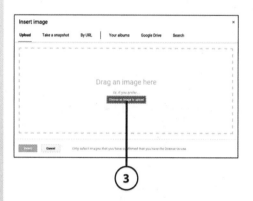

6. The image is now inserted in the slide. Use the touchpad to drag the image to a new location on the slide, if necessary.

7. To resize the image, click and drag the image's corner handles.

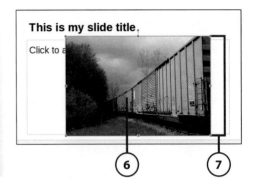

Changing the Look and Feel of a Presentation

Few people want to give a presentation of black text on a plain white background. You gain more attention by using attractive background colors and graphics.

Choose a New Theme

Google Slides lets you choose from several predesigned themes for your presentations. A *theme* is a predesigned collection of background images, color scheme, and fonts that are applied to every slide in your presentation.

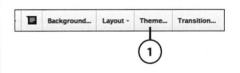

1. Click the Theme button in the toolbar to display the Choose a Theme panel.

2. Click the theme you want to use.

3. Click the OK button. The selected theme is now applied to all the slides in your presentation.

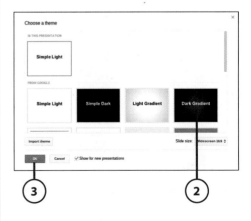

Add Custom Background Colors and Graphics

If you don't like the looks of any of Google Slides' predesigned themes, you can apply a custom background color or graphic to any or all the slides in your presentation.

1. Click the Background button on the toolbar to display the Background dialog box.

2. Click the Color control to select a different background color.

3. To use a background image, click the Choose button in the Image section and then select an image.

4. To apply this background to the current slide only, click the Done button.

5. To apply this background to all the slides in your presentation, click the Apply to All button.

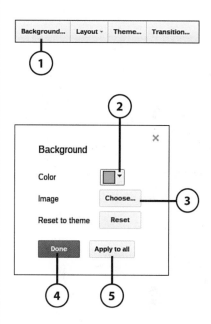

Using Transitions and Animations

To add visual interest to a presentation, add transitions between slides. You can also animate how individual elements appear on a given slide.

Add Transitions Between Slides

Google Slides offers a variety of transitions you can apply between slides, including fade, slide from right, slide from left, flip, cube, and gallery.

1. In the slide sorter pane, click the slide to which you wish to add a transition.

2. Click the Transition button on the toolbar to display the Animations pane.

3. Click the Transition Type button and select the desired transition.

4. Click and drag the slider to adjust the speed of the transition, from slow to fast.

5. To apply this transition to this slide only, click the X to close the Animations pane.

6. To apply this transition to all the slides in your presentation, click the Apply to All Slides button.

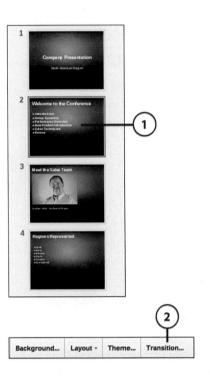

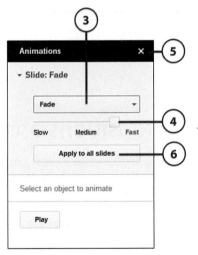

Animate Elements on a Slide

You can also animate the individual elements on a slide. That is, you can configure one element to appear after another element, via what Google calls *incremental reveal*.

When you choose to incrementally reveal an object, it doesn't appear when you first display the slide during a presentation. To reveal an object, you press the "next" button as if you were going to a new slide; this displays the first object chosen to reveal. If more than one object on a slide is formatted for incremental reveal, each successive object is displayed each time you press the "next" button.

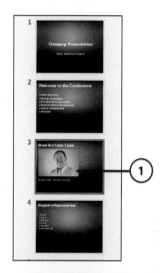

1. In the slide sorter pane, click the slide to which you wish to add animation.

2. On the slide, right-click the item you want to appear first.

3. From the pop-up menu, click Animate. This displays the Animations pane with this object selected.

4. Click the Animation Type button and select the type of animation you want for this item.

5. Click the Start Condition button and select the trigger for this animation—On Click, After Previous, or With Previous.

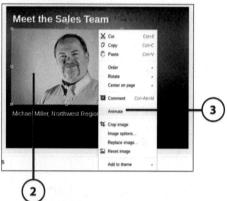

Animating Text

If you're animating text, and you want each paragraph (or bulleted/numbered line) to appear separately, check the By Paragraph option.

6. Click and drag the slider to adjust the speed of the animation, from slow to fast.

7. To animate the next object on the slide, select that object on the slide. The Animations pane remains open.

8. In the Animations pane, click Add Animation and then repeat steps 4 through 6.

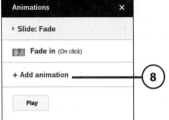

Giving Live Presentations

Of course, the main reason to create a presentation is to present it to others—which you can do from your Chromebook.

Present Your Presentation

Google Slides makes it easy to give presentations. After you've created and edited your presentation, you can connect your Chromebook to a projector or large monitor and show it to any sized group of people. In fact, you can take your presentation anywhere you travel just by connecting your computer to the Internet—where your presentation is stored.

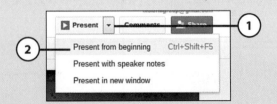

1. From within your presentation, click the down arrow next to the Present button.

2. Click Present from Beginning.

3. Your presentation now appears full screen, with a small control panel in the bottom-left corner. To advance to the next slide in the presentation, click the next-slide (right) arrow or press the right-arrow key on your keyboard.

4. If a slide includes objects formatted with incremental reveal, only the slide background and immediate reveal objects will appear when the slide first displays. To reveal the next object on the slide, click the next-slide arrow or press the right-arrow key on your keyboard.

5. When the presentation is finished, click Exit.

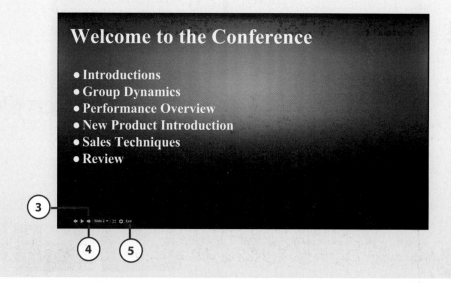

Printing and Sharing Presentations

You have a number of ways to share a presentation you create in Google Slides, including printing a hard copy and sharing online, via the Web.

Print Presentation Notes

Printing within Google Slides is handled by Google's Cloud Print service—which means you have to have Cloud Print configured before you start to print. (Learn more in Chapter 18, "Printing with Google Cloud Print.") You can use Google Cloud Print to create presentation notes for yourself or to hand out to your audience.

1. From within the presentation, click the File menu.

2. Click Print Settings and Preview.

3. This displays the preview panel. Click the second button on the toolbar and select what you want to print—1 slide with notes, 1 slide without notes, or handouts with 1, 2, 3, 4, 6, or 9 slides per page.

4. Click the Print button to display the Google Cloud Print panel.

5. If the Destination is not the printer you want, click the Change button and select a different printer.

6. Click the Print button.

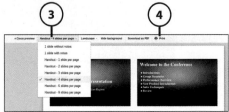

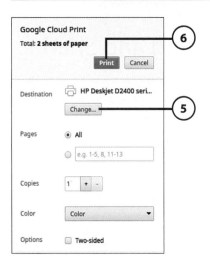

Share a Presentation with Others

Sharing a Google Slides presentation is similar to sharing any file on Google Drive. You have the option of letting others only view the shared presentation or edit it—the latter of which is what you want if you're collaborating on a group project.

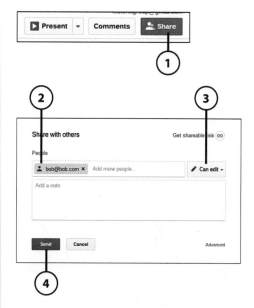

1. From within the presentation you want to share, click the Share button to display the Share with Others pane.

2. Enter the names or email addresses of the people you want to share this presentation with into the People box. Separate multiple names or email addresses with commas.

3. Click the button to the right of the People box and select whether these people Can Edit, Can Comment, or Can View this presentation.

4. Click the Send button, and the presentation is shared with those selected people.

Cloud Print-enabled printer

In this chapter, you learn how to use Google Cloud Print to print documents from your Chromebook.

18

Printing with Google Cloud Print

Printing from Chrome OS is substantially different than printing from Microsoft Windows or the Mac OS. It's more like printing from an iPad or other tablet—you can't.

That's because like iOS and other tablet operating systems, Chrome OS doesn't have a native printing function. Instead, it uses a new service, called Google Cloud Print, to print over the Internet to supported printers.

This means that your printing choices may be somewhat limited; you need a printer that's compatible with Google Cloud Print, or access to a normal printer connected to a Windows or Mac PC. Once everything's set up, printing is as simple as clicking a "print" button—only the setup is different.

Understanding Google Cloud Print

One of the things that makes Chrome OS different from other computer operating systems is that it doesn't carry with it a lot of legacy overhead—that is, the need to support older devices. That's one of the problems with Windows, for example; a large amount of programming code, disk space, and memory space is used to support thousands of printers and other devices from years past.

Google doesn't have that problem with Chrome OS; as a brand-new operating system, there are no older devices to support. And Google takes this approach even further, by choosing to not directly support all of the current printers available today.

Instead, Google has embraced a new technology dubbed Google Cloud Print. With this technology, Chrome is compatible with just a single device driver that is associated with the Cloud Print service. It's this service that then connects to various printers, reducing the load on the operating system.

The way Google Cloud Print works is simple. When you launch the "print" function in Chrome, the OS sends the print command over the Internet to the designated Cloud Print printer. The printer isn't physically connected to your Chromebook; the entire process is web based.

But what do you do if you have a printer without built-in Cloud Print capability, such as many older printers? Here, Google relies on other computers in your household or business. Cloud Print can print to any existing printer, as long as it's connected to a Windows or Mac computer that has Internet access. That is, Cloud Print relies on the PC for the connection—which means you have to have a Windows or Mac computer handy (and powered up).

The nice thing about Google Cloud Print is that you can use it to print from just about any device. Yes, you can print from your Chromebook to a Cloud Print printer, but you can also print from your iPhone or Android smartphone, your tablet, as well as from a Windows or Mac computer. And you can print from any location to any configured Cloud Print printer—which means you can be sitting in a hotel room in New York City and print to your Cloud Print printer back home in Omaha. No cables or printer drivers are necessary.

Connecting a Printer to Google Cloud Print

Before you can print from Google Chrome, you first must connect your printer to the Google Cloud Print service. You can connect either Cloud Print–ready printers or existing printers connected to a Windows or Mac computer.

Connect a Cloud Print-Ready Computer

If you're looking for a Cloud Print–ready printer, models are available from all major manufacturers. To use one of these printers for cloud printing, you must register it with the Google Cloud Print service. Follow your manufacturer's instructions to do so. (It's typically as simple as going to a registration page on the Web and entering your printer's email address.)

Connect an Existing Printer

To connect an existing printer to the Google Cloud Print service, it must be connected to a Windows or Mac computer that is connected to the Internet. The computer must also be running the Google Chrome web browser. You then enable the Google Cloud Print Connector, which con-nects this computer's printers to the Cloud Print service.

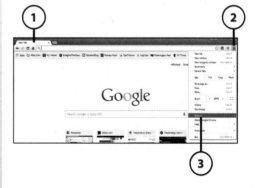

1. On your Windows or Mac computer, open the Google Chrome browser and, if necessary, sign in to your Google Account.

2. In the Chrome browser, click the Customize and Control button to display the drop-down menu.

3. Click Settings.

4. When the Settings page appears, scroll to the bottom of the page and click Show Advanced Settings; then go to the Google Cloud Print section and click the Manage button.

5. When the Devices page appears, go to the Classic Printers section and click the Add Printers button. (If your printer has already been added, you will not see this button.)

6. You now see all printers connected either directly or indirectly (over your home network) to this computer. Check those printers you want to add to the Cloud Print service.

7. Click the Add Printer(s) button to add the selected printers to the Cloud Print service.

Disconnect a Printer from Cloud Print

You can, at any time, remove a printer from the Google Cloud Print service.

1. From within Chrome, go to https://www.google.com/cloudprint/manage.html.

2. Click the Printers tab on the left.

3. Click the printer you want to disconnect.

4. Click the Delete button.

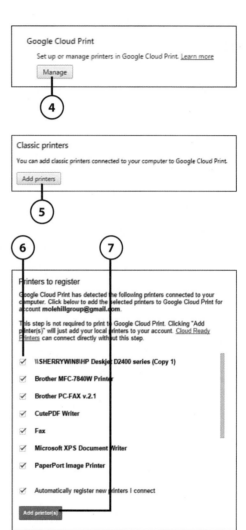

Printing to Google Cloud Print

Once you've registered a printer with the Google Cloud Print service, printing from your Chromebook is as easy as clicking a button. In fact, you can print from any computer, smartphone, or other device to that printer; all you need to do is provide your Google Account information.

Print from Your Chromebook

To print from your Chromebook to a printer connected to Google Cloud Print, that printer must be powered on and connected to the Internet. If it's a "classic" printer, it must also be connected to a Windows or Mac PC that is connected to the Internet.

1. From within Chrome, open the web page or application document you want to print.

2. Press Ctrl+P, or click the Customize and Control button and select Print.

3. When the Google Cloud Print panel appears, go to the Destination section and click the Change button to select the printer you want to use.

4. To print more than one copy, enter a number into the Copies box.

5. When you're ready to print, click the Print button.

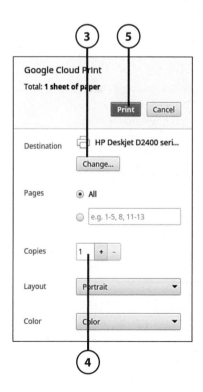

Sharing a Printer

After you've registered a printer with the Google Cloud Print service, you can then opt to let other users share that printer. You can share a Cloud Print printer with any user who has a Google Account.

Share a Printer

To share a printer with another user, you have to tell Google Cloud Print that the user has permission to print.

1. From within Chrome, go to https://www.google.com/cloudprint/manage.html.

2. Click the Printers tab on the left.

3. Click the printer you want to share.

4. Click the Share button.

5. When the Sharing Settings dialog box appears, enter the email address or username of the person you want to share with into the large box at the bottom.

6. Click the Share button.

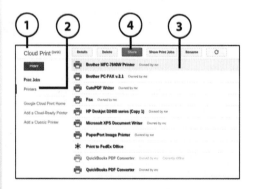

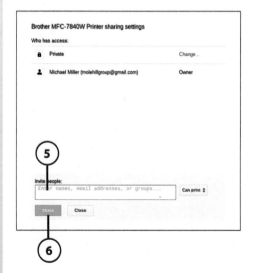

Disable Sharing

If, at a later date, you decide you no longer wish to share your printer with a particular user, you can delete that person from your approved sharing list.

1. From within Chrome, go to https://www.google.com/cloudprint/manage.html.

2. Click the Printers tab on the left.

3. Click the printer you want to *not* share.

4. Click the Share button.

5. When the Sharing Settings dialog box appears, go to the Permissions list and click the X next to that person's name.

6. Click the Close button.

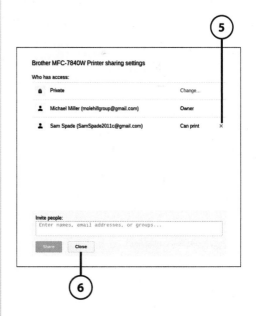

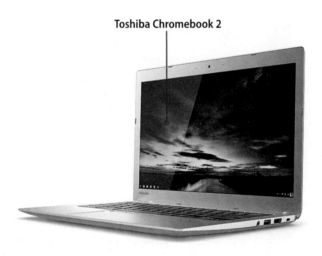
Toshiba Chromebook 2

In this chapter, you learn how to make your Chromebook run more efficiently, as well as how to deal with potential problems.

19

Optimizing and Troubleshooting Your Chromebook

How do you keep your Chromebook operating in tip-top condition? It's a matter of working safely and smartly, optimizing a handful of settings, and knowing what to do when things go wrong.

Using Chrome Safely and Securely

Many users are embracing Chromebooks because of security issues. That is, using a Chromebook with web-based storage is safer and more secure than using a traditional PC with local storage. You don't have to worry about computer viruses, spyware, and such; you don't

even have to worry about someone hacking into your computer and stealing your data.

This security inherent in the Chrome model is great, but there are things you can do to make your Chromebook even more safe and secure. It's a matter of practicing safe computing—and knowing all your options.

Chrome OS and Malware

Why are Chromebooks more secure than Windows or Mac computers? It's simple; because your Chromebook can't download, store, or run traditional applications, that also means it can't download malware—at all.

With a Chromebook, unlike any other form of personal computer, there's absolutely zero chance you'll run into computer viruses, spyware, and the like. Apple may talk about having less malware than Windows, but you can still hack into the Mac OS. You simply can't hack into Chrome OS; there's nothing on your Chromebook to infect.

So with a Chromebook you *don't* have to install antivirus, anti-spyware, or firewall programs. These tools aren't necessary because a Chromebook simply can't download and run malware programs. In fact, your Chromebook can't download executable programs of any type, so you're extremely safe from this sort of attack. There are no viruses, spyware, or other infiltrations possible with the Chrome OS.

Chromebooks Are Safe
Bottom line: There's no safer computer out there than a Chromebook.

Protect Against Phishing

Although Chrome OS and your Chromebook are, by design, virtually invulnerable to malware-based attacks, there's still the issue of those intrusions that depend on the human element to succeed. That is, when it comes to online scams, your Chromebook can't protect you from yourself.

One of the most common forms of online scams involves something called *phishing*, where a fraudster tries to extract valuable information from you via a series of fake email messages and websites.

Most phishing scams start with an email message. A phishing email is designed to look like an official email, but is in reality a clever forgery, down to the use of the original firm's logo. The goal of the email is to get you to click an enclosed link that purports to take you to an "official" website. That website, however, is also fake. Any information you provide to that website is then used for various types of fraud, from simple username/password theft to credit card and identity theft.

Of course, there's little Google can do to protect you from yourself; the best defense against phishing scams is simple common sense. That is, you should never click through a link in an email message that asks for any type of personal information—whether that be your bank account number or eBay password or whatever. Even if the email *looks* official, it probably isn't; legitimate institutions and websites never include this kind of link in their official messages. If you don't click to the phishing site, you're safe.

Fortunately, Google Chrome includes anti-phishing technology that can detect most phishing websites. If you navigate to a known phishing website, Chrome displays a warning message instead of the suspect web page. When you see this warning message in the Chrome browser, navigate away from the troublesome web page as quickly as possible.

Don't Save Passwords

By default, Chrome will offer to save the passwords you use to log on to various websites. However, if another user logs on to your Chromebook using your Google Account, they'll be able to access these password-protected sites without your knowledge or permission. It's safer, then, to *not* have Chrome save passwords.

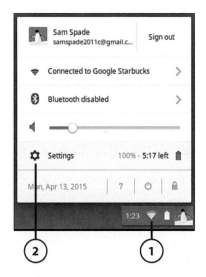

1. Click anywhere in the status area to display the Settings panel.

2. Click Settings to display the Settings page.

3. Click Show Advanced Settings; then scroll down to the Passwords and Forms section and *uncheck* the Offer to Save Your Web Passwords option.

Don't Use Autofill

Similarly, Chrome's Autofill feature will automatically save the personal data you enter into web forms for later automatic entry. If you want to be sure that other unauthorized users don't have access to this web form data, you'll want to turn off the Autofill feature.

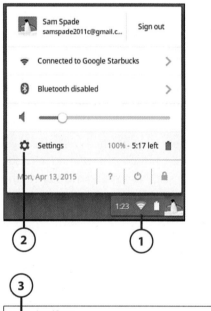

1. Click anywhere in the status area to display the Settings panel.

2. Click Settings to display the Settings page.

3. Click Show Advanced Settings; then scroll down to the Passwords and Forms section and *uncheck* the Enable Autofill to Fill Out Web Forms in a Single Click option.

Configure Privacy Settings

Chrome OS includes a bevy of small but important privacy settings you can configure to increase your online privacy. These are detailed in the following table.

Google Chrome Privacy Settings

Setting	Description	Recommendation
Use a web service to help resolve navigation errors.	When this feature is enabled, Google will suggest alternate pages if you encounter an incorrect or nonworking URL.	When enabled, this feature sends every URL you enter to Google, where it could be stored and used for other purposes. Google doesn't need to do this, and you can figure out your own errors; for increased privacy, disable this setting.
Use a prediction service to help complete searches and URLs typed in the Address bar or the App Launcher search box.	By default, Google suggests queries when you start typing a search into Chrome's Omnibox.	Because this feature sends a detailed history of your web searching to Google, you can increase your privacy by disabling this setting—and not letting Google track your search behavior.
Prefetch resources to load pages more quickly	When this feature is enabled, Google "prefetches" all the URLs on each web page you load, essentially looking them up in advance, in the event you click them. This should speed up the loading of any subsequent pages you click to.	This is a fairly harmless option, at least in terms of privacy. Because it can, in theory, speed up your browsing, it's a good option to enable.
Automatically report details of possible security incidents to Google.	This feature helps Google better detect files and sites that are harmful or unsafe.	This feature only sends data to Google when Chrome detects a suspicious website or download. Although the intent is good, it still can be used to track your online behavior, so you may want to disable it.
Enable phishing and malware protection.	Google's anti-phishing protection works by comparing the URLs you enter with a database of known phishing URLs.	Although Chrome may send some subset of the URL you enter to Google, Google never sees the full URL, and doesn't track your browsing history. Because of the valuable protection offered, this is a good feature to keep enabled.

Setting	Description	Recommendation
Use a web service to help resolve spelling errors.	This setting adds spell checking to Chrome, using the same spell-checking technology employed by Google search.	When this option is enabled, anything you type into the Chrome browser is sent to Google's servers for evaluation. Not only can this slow down your browsing, it's also sending more personal data to Google. Best not to enable.
Automatically send usage statistics and crash reports to Google.	By default, Google will receive reports about how you use Chrome and what you're doing if and when the browser crashes.	Usage statistics and crash reports? That means Google receives a copy of everything you do in Chrome. You can increase your privacy by disabling this setting and not letting Google track all your actions.
Send a "Do Not Track" request with your browsing traffic.	This technology lets you opt out of tracking by websites you don't actually visit—advertising networks, analytic services, and the like.	When you enable this option, you get fewer entities tracking your web browsing—which is a good thing, privacy-wise.
Enable Verified Access.	Verified Access enables your Chromebook to certify that certain cryptographic keys are protected by the Chrome hardware. To do this, Verified Access sends hardware information to a Google server.	When this setting is activated, Google's server can identify your Chromebook, although it can't identify you as a user. You should disable this setting unless you're using a Chromebook supplied by an employer that uses the Verified Access feature.

1. Click anywhere in the status area to display the Settings panel.
2. Click Settings to display the Settings page.
3. Click Show Advanced Settings; then scroll down to the Privacy section and uncheck any settings you don't want to use.

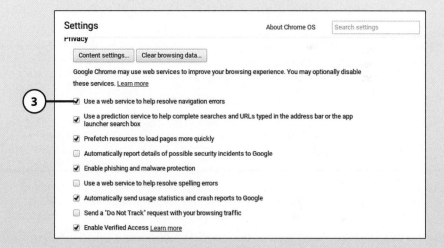

Configure Content Settings

Chrome also includes more than a dozen settings that determine what content is displayed in the browser. The following table details these settings.

Google Chrome Content Settings

Setting	Description	Recommendation
Cookies	Cookies are small files that websites store on your computer to track your browsing behavior. You can opt to allow cookies (default) or block all cookies. You can also allow cookies except from third-party sites or clear cookies when you close your browser.	As onerous as cookies sound, they help make it easier to revisit your favorite sites. However, you can increase your privacy by blocking all cookies, or by clearing cookies when you close your browser (log off from Chrome). Know, however, that without cookies, you'll need to re-enter all your personal data each time you visit a website.
Images	You can opt to show all images on web pages, or not show any images.	Not showing images will speed up web browsing, but decrease the usability of many sites.
JavaScript	JavaScript is a kind of programming language used to create certain website content. Unfortunately, JavaScript can be used to run malicious scripts in your browser—although that's much less likely or dangerous in the Chrome OS.	Although you can increase security by not running JavaScript, this can make some websites less functional. Because Chrome OS is fairly protected against malicious code, this setting is probably safe to leave enabled.
Handlers	Handlers enable websites to perform certain actions when links on their sites are clicked.	By default, sites are allowed to ask you if you want to perform a certain action when a link is clicked. You can disable this functionality and block all such requests.
Plug-ins	You can increase the functionality of your browser, and of certain websites, by running plug-in software.	Most plug-ins are harmless. If you're concerned about security, you can disable this setting—although some sites may not run as advertised.
Pop-ups	Pop-up windows are a particularly pernicious form of unwanted online advertising. Most people hate them.	You can make your web browsing less annoying by letting Chrome block all pop-ups. (This is the default setting.)
Location	Some websites can serve up a more personalized experience if they know where you're located.	Do you really want all the sites you visit to know where you are? You can increase your privacy by turning off location tracking, or at least forcing sites to ask you before they track.

Notifications	Some websites display desktop notifications of various activities.	By default, a site has to ask for permission to display notifications. You can opt to allow or not allow such notifications.
Fullscreen	Some websites request to open in fullscreen mode.	You can choose how Chrome handles fullscreen requests.
Mouse Cursor	Some websites or web apps (games, in particular) may request to disable your Chromebook's mouse cursor.	You can choose how Chrome handles this type of request.
Protected Content	Some sites and services use machine identifiers to uniquely identify your computer in order to authorize access to protected content such as movies or music that you've purchased.	By default, these types of identifiers are allowed. You can turn off this setting, however, or allow exceptions to the general rule.
Media	Sites with media functionality can request access to your Chromebook's webcam and microphone.	You can select which media devices to use, as well as disallow all such access.
Unsandboxed Plug-in Access	Chrome's sandbox mode protects your computer by limiting what websites can access your computer.	By default, sites can ask to use a plug-in to access your computer. You can allow or disallow all such requests.
Automatic Downloads	These controls affect how files are downloaded on your Chromebook.	By default, a site must ask to download files automatically (after the first file). You can allow or disallow this type of automatic file downloading.
Zoom Levels	Some websites may seek to control the zoom level on your Chromebook screen.	You can manage which sites are allowed/disallowed to control this function.

1. Click anywhere in the status area to display the Settings panel.
2. Click Settings to display the Settings page.

3. Click Show Advanced Settings; scroll down to the Privacy section and click the Content Settings button.

4. When the Content Settings panel appears, select or deselect the desired settings.
5. Click the Done button when done.

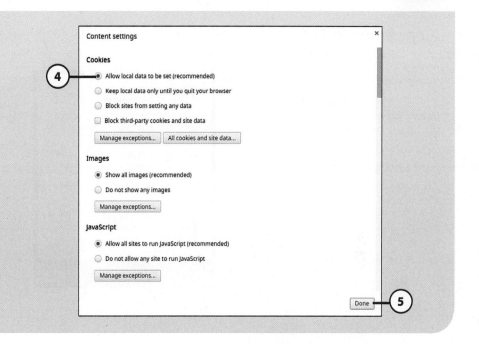

Clear Browsing Data

If you want to cover your tracks, as it were, you can clear the data that Chrome keeps about your browsing history. In particular, you can do the following:

- Clear browsing history

- Clear download history

- Empty the cache

- Delete cookies and other site data

- Clear saved passwords

- Clear saved Autofill form data

1. Click anywhere in the status area to display the Settings panel.

2. Click Settings to display the Settings page.

3. Click Show Advanced Settings; scroll down to the Privacy section and click the Clear Browsing Data button.

4. When the Clear Browsing Data dialog box appears, check those items you wish to clear or delete.

5. Pull down the list and select how much data (for how long) you wish to clear.

6. Click the Clear Browsing Data button.

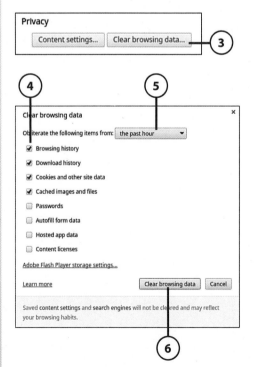

Restrict Sign-In

There's one last setting you should consider. By default, anyone with a Google Account can log in to your Chromebook, and then log in to their own personal data and settings. You may not want just anyone to use your Chromebook, however; to that end, you can limit use to only those people you preselect.

1. Click anywhere in the status area to display the Settings panel.

2. Click Settings to display the Settings page.

3. Go to the People section and click the Manage Other Users button.

4. Check the Restrict Sign-In to the Following Users option.

5. Enter the email addresses of those people you want to use your Chromebook into the Add Users box and then press Enter.

6. Click the Done button.

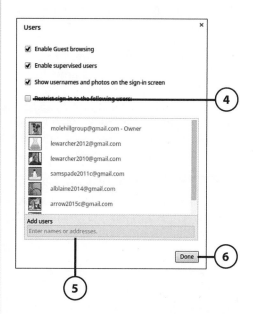

Optimizing Your Chromebook's Performance

Out of the box, a Chromebook is a very fast computer with a very long battery life. There are things you can do, however, to make it run ever faster—and last longer on a charge.

Optimize Battery Life

Let's start with your Chromebook's battery life. On average, you're going to get 8–10 hours per charge, depending on the model, which is pretty good. Your battery may last longer, however, if you take the appropriate precautions:

- **Use the right adapter.** Use only the charger/adapter supplied by your Chromebook's manufacturer, or an authorized replacement. Using the wrong charger/adapter can negatively impact the life of your battery—or even damage the Chromebook itself.

- **Keep it cool.** Batteries don't like heat. The hotter the room, the less the battery will hold its charge—and the increased likelihood you'll damage the Chromebook. Worst-case scenario, your Chromebook will get hot enough to catch fire. This is not desirable. It's best, then, to keep your Chromebook as near room temperature as possible, even when it's not in use.

- **Keep a little charge.** When you're not using your Chromebook for an extended period, charge the battery to about the 30%–40% level. This level of charge will maintain battery performance as best as possible.

- **Dim the screen.** When running your Chromebook on battery power, turn down the screen brightness. A brighter screen draws more power, and runs the battery down faster.

- **Disable Wi-Fi.** If you're not working online, turn off Wi-Fi functionality. Your Chromebook's wireless receiver draws a lot of power. (Of course, your Chromebook is fairly useless if not connected to the Internet, so this may not be a viable option.)

>>>Go Further

BATTERY REPLACEMENT

All batteries get weaker over time. If your battery life starts to deteriorate, or if your battery stops working altogether, you'll need to replace it with a new battery.

Unfortunately, the battery is sealed into your Chromebook; it's not user replaceable. To remove or replace your Chromebook's internal battery, you'll need to take it or send it to an authorized service center.

Speed Up Performance

On a traditional computer, you can speed up performance by managing how programs use the PC's memory and hard disk. Because most Chromebooks don't have hard disks, there isn't much to manage there—which is one of the reasons a Chromebook is so fast by default.

There are a few things you can do, however, to speed up the performance of your Chromebook. Because most of what you do will be web based, most of these tricks involve how you browse online:

- **Don't multitask.** Each web app that's running takes up processor capacity, memory, and upload/download bandwidth. If multiple apps are running simultaneously, in multiple browser tabs or windows, that can really slow down your Chromebook's processing—and clog up your Internet connection. This can even be the case if some of those apps are running in the background, like a real-time weather or stock app. Bottom line, if you don't want your Chromebook to become too sluggish, close some of those browser tabs.

- **Disable or remove extensions.** Similarly, the Chrome extensions you install can create a drain on your memory and processing power. The more little buttons you have on the Chrome toolbar, the more things your Chromebook has to run. Speed things up by disabling or removing those extensions you don't really need or use, as discussed in Chapter 10, "Using Chrome Apps and Extensions."

- **Disable DNS prefetching.** When configured properly, the Chrome browser can "prefetch" all the URLs on each web page you load, essentially looking them up in advance in the event you click them. This speeds up the loading of any subsequent pages you click to, which results in faster browsing. To enable DNS prefetching, open the Settings page, click Show Advanced Settings, go to the Privacy section, and check the Prefetch Resources to Load Pages More Quickly option.

- **Disable feedback to Google.** Several configuration settings send information to Google for further action. Forgetting for the moment the privacy implications of these operations, they can slow down your web browsing—especially if you're on a slow connection. Data you send upstream to Google can clog up the pipeline for the data you need to flow downstream. In particular, you may want to consider disabling the following privacy settings: Use a web service to help resolve navigation errors; Use a prediction service to help complete searches and URLs typed into the Address bar or the App Launcher search box; Enable phishing and malware protection; and Automatically send usage statistics and crash reports to Google.

Troubleshooting Chromebook Problems

Your Chromebook is much more reliable than a traditional personal computer. The lack of any moving parts (no hard drive or optical drive) enhances reliability, and the technical compactness of Chrome OS (no legacy stuff to support) means there's less stuff to go wrong.

That doesn't mean you'll never encounter any problems, however; there are still times when a particular app or web page or even your entire Chromebook might freeze. Fortunately, your Chromebook's inherent simplicity makes it easy to troubleshoot and recover from even the most significant issues.

Deal with a Frozen App or Web Page

Perhaps the most common problem you're likely to encounter is a frozen application or web page—that is, the tab you're currently on doesn't respond to anything you do. Sometimes you can navigate off this tab to another tab or window, sometimes not; but in any case you're left with one nonresponsive tab.

When this happens, you can undertake the following steps, in order, to close the tab and resume your other work.

1. Start by simply trying to close the tab. Click the X on the tab itself, or select the tab and then press Ctrl+W (or do both).

2. If the tab is still frozen, you can try shutting down the window it's in by pressing Ctrl+Shift+W. (This only works if you have more than one window open.)

3. If that doesn't work, press Shift+Esc (or click the Customize and Control button and select More Tools, Task Manager) to open the Chrome Task Manager. All running tasks (apps, pages, extensions, and so forth) are listed in the Task Manager window. To close the frozen task, click that task and then click the End Process button.

Task Manager

Chrome OS features a Task Manager, similar to the one in Microsoft Windows. You use the Task Manager to review all running tasks and services—and to shut down tasks that won't close of their own accord.

4. If the tab still won't close, you need to shut down and then restart your Chromebook. Press and hold the Power button for about 8 seconds until your Chromebook completely powers off—then restart your Chromebook and get back to work.

Reset Your Chromebook

Although most of the data you use on your Chromebook is stored in the cloud, some personal data (primarily about user accounts) is stored locally. Sometimes this locally stored data can become corrupted, causing your Chromebook to misbehave.

When this happens, you can often get things working again by resetting your Chromebook to its original condition—what Google calls *power-washing*. This in effect clears all your local data from the Chromebook, leaving you with a factory-fresh machine.

1. Click anywhere in the status area to display the Settings panel.

2. Click Settings to display the Settings page.

3. Scroll to the bottom of the page and click Show Advanced Settings.

4. Go to the Powerwash section and then click the Powerwash button.

5. When the Restart Your Device dialog box appears, click the Restart button.

6. This restarts your Chromebook, with all local data deleted. Follow the instructions in online Chapter 20, "Unboxing and Setting Up Your New Chromebook," to create a new user account and set up your Chromebook from scratch.

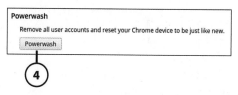

Reset from the Sign-In Screen

You can also reset your Chromebook from the sign-in screen. Just press Ctrl+Alt+Shift+R and then click Restart.

It's Not All Good

When you reset your Chromebook, you not only clear usernames and logon information, you also delete any other data saved on your Chromebook. This includes photos, downloaded files, saved networks, and the like. All data for all accounts is deleted. The next time you start up your Chromebook will be just like the first time; you'll be prompted to create a new user account, and so forth.

>>>Go Further

UPDATING CHROME OS

One of the nice things about Chrome OS is that it automatically updates itself every time it's turned on. That is, when you power up your Chromebook, Chrome goes online to check for updates; if any are available, they're automatically downloaded and installed at that point.

If Chrome detects a new update while you're using your Chromebook, you can manually update Chrome OS at that point, without waiting for the next time you shut down and then restart your machine. All you have to do is click within the status area to display the Settings panel and then click Restart to Update.

Chrome now downloads the update and restarts your Chromebook. Log back in as normal to resume work.

Google Chrome Keyboard Shortcuts

A *keyboard shortcut* is a combination of two or more keyboard buttons that you use to perform specific actions within Google Chrome. Using keyboard shortcuts can be a real time saver.

Navigation and Browser Shortcuts

Keyboard Shortcut	Action
Ctrl+Alt+/	Display list of keyboard shortcuts
Ctrl+O	Open a file
Alt+Shift+M	Open the Files app
Shift+Esc	Open Task Manager
Ctrl+H	Open History page
Ctrl+J	Open Downloads page
Alt+E	Open Customize and Control menu
Ctrl+Shift+B	Toggle Bookmarks bar on or off
Ctrl+Full Screen	Configure external monitor

Ctrl+Alt+Z	Enable/disable accessibility settings (if you're not logged in to a Google Account)
Ctrl+Shift+Q	Sign out of your Google Account
Ctrl+?	Go to Help Center

Tab and Window Navigation Shortcuts

Keyboard Shortcut	Action
Ctrl+T	Open a new tab
Ctrl+W	Close the current tab
Ctrl+Shift+T	Reopen the last tab you closed
Ctrl+Tab	Go to next tab
Ctrl+Shift+Tab	Go to previous tab
Ctrl+1 through Ctrl+8	Go to the specified tab
Ctrl+9	Go to the last tab
Ctrl+N	Open a new window
Ctrl+Shift+N	Open a new window in Incognito mode
Ctrl+Shift+W	Close the current window
Alt+Tab	Go to next window
Alt+Shift+Tab	Go to previous window
Alt+1 through Alt+8	Go to the specified window
Alt+9	Go to the last open window
Alt+−	Minimize window
Alt+=	Maximize window
Alt+Shift and +	Center current window
Click and hold Back or Forward button in browser toolbar	See browsing history for that tab
Backspace or Alt+Left Arrow	Go to previous page in browsing history
Shift+Backspace or Alt+Right Arrow	Go to next page in browsing history
Ctrl+click a link	Open link in new tab in background
Ctrl+Shift+click a link	Open link in new tab in foreground
Shift+click a link	Open link in new window
Drag a link to a tab	Open link in the tab

Drag a link to a blank area on the tab strip	Open link in new tab
Type URL in Address bar and then press Alt+Enter	Open URL in new tab
Press Esc while dragging a tab	Return tab to its original position

Page Shortcuts

Keyboard Shortcut	Action
Alt+Up Arrow	Page up
Alt+Down Arrow	Page down
Spacebar	Scroll down web page
Ctrl+Alt+Up Arrow	Home
Ctrl+Alt+Down Arrow	End
Ctrl+P	Print page
Ctrl+S	Save page
Ctrl+R	Reload page
Ctrl+Shift+R	Reload page without using cached content
Esc	Stop loading current page
Ctrl and +	Zoom in
Ctrl and –	Zoom out
Ctrl+0	Reset zoom level
Ctrl+D	Save page as bookmark
Ctrl+Shift+D	Save all open pages in window as bookmarks in a new folder
Drag a link to Bookmarks bar	Save link as bookmark
Ctrl+F	Search current page
Ctrl+G or Enter	Go to next match for page search
Ctrl+Shift+G or Shift+Enter	Go to previous match for page search
Ctrl+K or Ctrl+E	Search Web
Ctrl+Enter	Add www. and .com to input in Address bar and open resulting URL
Ctrl+Next Window	Take a screenshot of current screen
Ctrl+U	View page source

Ctrl+Shift+I	Toggle display of Developer Tools panel
Ctrl+Shift+J	Toggle display of the DOM Inspector

Text Editing Shortcuts

Keyboard Shortcut	Description
Ctrl+A	Select everything on page
Ctrl+L or Alt+D	Select content in Omnibox
Ctrl+Shift+Right Arrow	Select next word or letter
Ctrl+Shift+Left Arrow	Select previous word or letter
Ctrl+Right Arrow	Move to start of next word
Ctrl+Left Arrow	Move to start of previous word
Ctrl+C	Copy selected content to clipboard
Ctrl+V	Paste content from clipboard
Ctrl+Shift+V	Paste content from clipboard as plain text
Ctrl+X	Cut
Ctrl+Backspace	Delete previous word
Alt+Backspace	Delete next letter
Ctrl+Z	Undo last action

Index

G

Q–R

REGISTER THIS PRODUCT
SAVE 35%*
ON YOUR NEXT PURCHASE!

How to Register Your Product

- Go to quepublishing.com/register
- Sign in or create an account
- Enter ISBN: 10- or 13-digit ISBN that appears on the back of the book.

Benefits of Registering

- Ability to download product updates
- Access to bonus chapters and workshop files
- A 35% coupon to be used on your next purchase – valid for 30 days
  > To obtain your coupon, click on "Manage Codes" in the right column of your Account page
- Receive special offers on new editions and related Que products

Please note that the benefits for registering may vary by product. Benefits will be listed on your Account page under Registered Products.

We value and respect your privacy. Your email address will not be sold to any third party company.

* 35% discount code presented after product registration is valid on most print books, eBooks, and full-course videos sold on QuePublishing.com. Discount may not be combined with any other offer and is not redeemable for cash. Discount code expires after 30 days from the time of product registration. Offer subject to change.

quepublishing.com